Mathematical Applications in
Political Science
V

Mathematical
Applications
in Political Science
V

Edited by James F. Herndon and Joseph L. Bernd

Virginia Polytechnic Institute
and State University

The University Press of Virginia

Charlottesville

THE UNIVERSITY PRESS OF VIRGINIA

Copyright © 1971 by the Rector and Visitors
of the University of Virginia

First published 1971

Standard Book Number: 8139–0313–0
Library of Congress Catalog Card Number: 67–28023
Printed in the United States of America

Contents

Introduction / *James F. Herndon and Joseph L. Bernd*   1

1 A Model of Social Interaction / *Gordon Tullock*   4

2 Some Decisions in the Regression Analysis of Time-Series
   Data / *Bruce M. Russett*   29

3 Spatial Models for the Analysis of Roll-Call Data / *Duncan
   MacRae, Jr.*   51

4 Compound Paths in Political Analysis / *Donald E. Stokes*   70

Tables

2.1 Simultaneous relationships between defense and civil spending, and relationships with a one-year lag   36

2.2 Model A—relationships between levels of defense and civil spending   44

2.3 Model B—relationships between changes in defense and civil spending   45

2.4 Model C—relationships between percentage changes in defense and civil spending   46

2.5 Comparison of models A and B with two-independent variable equations, 1939–68   49

Figures

1.1 Individual choice   6

1.2 Choice on a continuum   11

1.3 Democracy and despotism   15

1.4 Party politics   17

1.5 Choice with payments   19

1.6 Revolt against a despotism   22

1.7 Choice within a party   26

2.1 Defense expenditures as a percentage of U.S. GNP,
      1939–68   39

3.1 Thirty artificial points with twenty-six cutting lines   56

3.2 Factor loadings for artificial data from Q-matrix   58

3.3 Factor scores for artificial data from Q-matrix   59

3.4 Factor loadings for artificial data from ϕ-matrix   60

3.5 Factor scores for artificial data from ϕ-matrix   61

3.6 Analyses of artificial data by Guttman-Lingoes Smallest
      Space Analysis   63

Mathematical Applications in
Political Science
V

Introduction

James F. Herndon and Joseph L. Bernd
Virginia Polytechnic Institute and
State University

THE papers collected in this volume were delivered originally in an institute in Mathematical Applications in Political Science supported by the National Science Foundation and conducted by Virginia Polytechnic Institute during the summer of 1969. The University Press of Virginia and the Extension Division of Virginia Polytechnic Institute have cooperated in publication of these papers. The volume takes its place with the four volumes of similar nature published earlier.[1]

If there is any theme common to the four papers presented here it is their authors' exploration of solutions to problems realized in the course of substantive research. The authors' concerns have to do both with techniques appropriate to the quantitative manipulation of data and the suitability of particular mathematical and conceptual models.

These are essentially problems of choice. Accordingly, our authors' arguments are frequently turned to the delineation of alternatives and the reasons for their preference of one over another. The data considered in the four papers serve principally an illustrative end, as demonstrations of the sorts of problems the investigator may have encountered or as examples of the applicability of the methods he has devised.

Our contributors' collective intent, if we may speak for them, is that of stimulating further exploration in methods and application in research of the approaches they discuss in these pages. We fully share that intent.

The first paper in the collection, Gordon Tullock's "A Model of Social Interaction," represents an effort to construct a relatively simple model capable of wide application by students of social behavior.

---

[1] John M. Claunch, ed., *Mathematical Applications in Political Science* (Dallas, 1965); Joseph L. Bernd, ed., *Mathematical Applications in Political Science II* (Dallas, 1966); Joseph L. Bernd, ed., *Mathematical Applications in Political Science III* (Charlottesville, 1967); and Joseph L. Bernd, ed., *Mathematical Applications in Political Science IV* (Charlottesville, 1969).

Based on the econometric models developed by Professor Tullock and others, the model presented here takes as its province a variety of choice situations and seeks to identify those variables common to each. The argument centers on the action costs to the chooser and the risks involved to those presenting the choice. Illustrations are drawn from such widely disparate situations as voting in a democratic election, criminal behavior, market exchange, revolution and riot, the Wars of the Roses, and the 1968 Democratic National Convention.

Bruce Russett's "Some Decisions in the Regression Analysis of Time-Series Data" is addressed to methodological problems encountered in his earlier analysis of which economic sectors contribute most to paying the costs of national defense. Professor Russett describes in some detail the alternatives open to him for handling his data and the reasons for having made the choices he did. Among his concerns are those of autocorrelation, simultaneous and lagged relationships, and the selection of data. Three separate models are derived and described, and reasons for preference among these are set down.

Recognizing the wide use of roll-call analysis, Duncan MacRae, Jr., argues for the importance of establishing a firm foundation for the techniques employed in such analysis. His "Spatial Models for the Analysis of Roll-Call Data" breaks new ground in its discussion of methods of moving from the one-dimensionality of conventional Guttman scale analysis to models of higher dimensionality. A least-cubes model for cumulative scales is developed here after Professor MacRae indicates results obtained from the application of other models (factor analysis and smallest-space analysis) to a set of artificial data.

Methods developed originally by students of population genetics are put to use by Donald E. Stokes in analyzing relationships of congressmen and their constituencies. In his paper "Compound Paths in Political Analysis," Professor Stokes describes the derivation and use of simultaneous equation methods in the investigation of multivariate systems. His paper concludes with a discussion of problems in measurement and research design which, if solved, will enable more extensive use of the model he presents in political research.

Duncan MacRae, Jr., is Professor of Political Science at the University of Chicago. He received the Ph.D. at Harvard University and has taught at Harvard, the University of California at Berkeley, and Princeton University. He has been a Fulbright research scholar in France. His writings include *Dimensions of Congressional Voting* (1958), *Parliament, Parties and Society in France, 1946–58* (1967), and *Issues and Parties in Legislative Voting: Methods of Statistical Analysis* (1969).

Bruce M. Russett is Director of the Yale University Political Data Program. A Yale Ph.D., Professor Russett has taught at Yale, Columbia University, and the Massachusetts Institute of Technology. His major publications include *World Handbook of Political and Social Indicators* (with Hayward R. Alker, Jr., Karl W. Deutsch, and Harold D. Lasswell, 1964), *Trends in World Politics* (1965), *International Regions and the International System* (1967), and *Economic Theories of International Politics* (1968).

Donald E. Stokes is Study Director, Survey Research Center, and Professor of Political Science at the University of Michigan. He has also taught at Yale University. Professor Stokes is coauthor of *The American Voter* (1960) and *Elections and the Political Order* (1966) as well as author and coauthor of a series of important articles and monographs on the American electorate.

Gordon Tullock is Professor of Economics and Public Choice at Virginia Polytechnic Institute and State University. He received the Juris Doctor at the University of Chicago in 1957 and has held teaching positions at Rice University and the University of Virginia. He is author of *A Practical Guide for Ambitious Politicians* (1961), *Calculus of Consent* (with James Buchanan, 1962), and *Toward a Mathematics of Politics* (1967). Professor Tullock is also editor of the journal *Public Choice.*

A Model of Social Interaction

1 Gordon Tullock
Virginia Polytechnic Institute and
State University

Introduction

It is the purpose of this paper to present and elaborate a general model which covers a very large number of categories of human action. It will, for example, cover market action, democratic political action, and political action in nondemocratic areas. Further, as we shall see, it permits explanation of certain aspects of democratic politics which do not seem to fit the existing theories of democracy.

In order to present this model, it is necessary first to look at the world in a rather unusual manner. Many modern economists have referred to the choice system as decisions among different states of the world. When I make a decision the world is different from what it would be if I made another choice. Thus, I am choosing between two states of the world. For example, I currently own a blue Plymouth which is about a year and a half old. I could trade this in on a new red Mustang with the result that my inventory would change both with respect to cars and to money and a local car dealer would have more money. Let us look at this problem in a somewhat more complex way. The existing state of the world can be represented by a point in a multidimensional space. One of these dimensions would be my cash balance; another would represent various characteristics of the car which I might have or do have. For example, the age of the car which I own might appear on one dimension, the manufacturer as a series of discontinuous points on another, and various other characteristics of the car on further axes. The *status quo* is one point in this multidimensional space, and I could be considering whether it would be desirable to move to another location, i.e., one in which I owned a red Mustang instead of my present blue Plymouth.

The model so far will seem familiar to most students of modern economics. I would like to change it, however, by adding one additional dimension. This additional dimension will cover the cost to any individual of entering into any transaction, and this cost will be called "action cost." We shall find, however, that variations along this additional dimension permit us to deal with many different types of social situation.

The presentation of this type of multidimensional space on two-dimensional paper is, strictly speaking, impossible. In the following sections, therefore, I shall compress all of the dimensions except the action-cost dimension into a single dimension. For our purposes, this simplification will be harmless. For those who do not like this simplification and are willing to pay the mathematical cost which is necessary to avoid it, the matrix model developed by Davis and Hinich [1] will permit direct discussion of the many-dimensional continuum which is characteristic of the real world. Further, I shall usually assume that most of the choices are simple choices between two alternatives. In the real world (and in some of our examples) choices tend to be more complicated. I feel, however, that the two alternative choices lead to no significant distortion.

As the game theorists have pointed out, action in the world can generally be analyzed as a sequence of moves. One party makes some decision or takes some action; this changes the world in some way, and other parties can then take action or make decisions which again affect the world. Our model will deal with such a sequence and will in each case simply inquire as to the type of action an individual would take at some state in the process. A collection of such individual actions, of course, would cover any real world situation. Further, in the main body of the essay we shall discuss only those situations in which the individual does not engage in bargaining or negotiation. Characteristic cases would be an individual deciding whether or not to buy, whether or not to vote, or whether or not to enter into a revolution; a company deciding what characteristics to give its car; a government deciding what its platform for the next election will be; or a despotism considering how large the budget for the secret police should be. The model can be fitted to bargaining, but a discussion of these situations will be postponed to another occasion. In general, the main body of the essay will be devoted to take it or leave it situations. This in general means situations in which individuals confront fairly large organizations or in some cases where fairly large organizations confront other fairly large organizations.

[1] Otto A. Davis and Melvin J. Hinich, "On the Power and Importance of the Mean Preference in a Mathematical Model of Democratic Choice," *Public Choice*, V (Fall, 1968), 59–72.

I. Individual Choice

On the vertical axis of Figure 1.1, I have a single-dimensional choice variable of some sort. It could, for example, be the horsepower of the automobile engine or any one of a large number of other things. It represents the total mass of possible alternatives. On this vertical axis I have the individual's optimum for this particular variable, and

Figure 1.1.   Individual choice

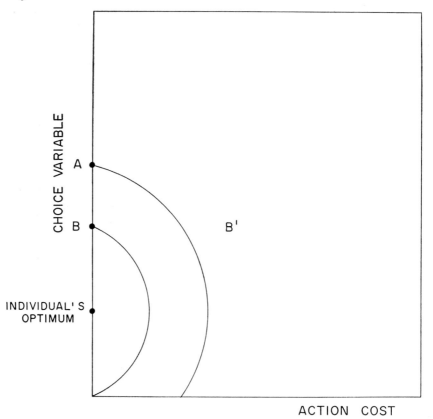

two choices, *A* and *B*, are also shown. *A* is the *status quo*, and *B* is a proposed change. For the next few paragraphs we will assume that all choices are between the *status quo* and a specific change. Later we will consider the situation in which a number of changes in the *status quo* are possible.

On the horizontal axis I have drawn in the action cost, the cost of making a definite choice. In ordinary economic activities, this cost is so tiny that we tend to ignore it. It would involve such things as actually telling the salesman that you want the car or telling him that you do not. Note that the gathering of information preliminary to making a choice is not included here in the cost of action. For the purposes of this particular paper, we shall assume that the individual would have indifference curves of the general shape shown. In the ordinary market, the actual cost of making decisions is very tiny, and so surely an individual would choose to move from the *status quo* to point *B* if this alternative were offered to him. If the *status quo* happened to be point *B*, and the alternative *A* were offered, he would refuse it.

What we have said so far is clearly a clumsy but accurate way of dealing with individual choice in the market. I have offered this model not simply in order to complicate the existing analysis of market choice but because this particular model can be adjusted to deal with many other types of choice. Note that most of the problems discussed in economic textbooks are eliminated in this model simply because a number of choice variables have been collapsed into one. If we had the manifold real world dimensional system, then the standard Edgeworth[2] box would show a pair of axes perpendicular to our action-cost axis. By shrinking these axes to one, we collapse most of these problems into the very simple choice problem between *A* and *B*. This model has never been used before, mainly, I presume, because the cost of choice is so small in most economic activities that we rarely if ever bother to discuss it.

The problem of crime has attracted very little attention from economists. The reason is probably that in crime there is characteristically no exchange. The individual simply takes what he wants. Crime is, however, as easily analyzable in our current model as is a market exchange. Let us say that I would like to acquire a red Mustang and do not intend to pay for it. I will simply seize that of my neighbor. It no doubt will involve a small amount of work on my part getting the car, but this is, generally speaking, trivial compared to the value of the car itself.

Society, however, has dealt with the problem of crime in general by making the cost of action quite high. Thus, if I steal my neighbor's car, I run a finite chance—something on the order of 1 in 50—of

---

[2] F. Y. Edgeworth was a distinguished mathematical economist of the late nineteenth century. His principal book is *Mathematical Psychics* (London: Kegan Paul, 1881).

spending two to three years in prison. If I discount this possibility of imprisonment appropriately and find that the results indicate the crime has a positive payoff, point B in Figure 1.1 for example, I would still be sensible if I stole the car. Of course, I would not be as sensible as if there were no "costs." On the other hand, if I computed the present discount value of a one-in-fifty chance of two years in prison as B', I would choose not to take the car.

We note here, immediately, that society has a fairly easy technique for influencing the number of crimes committed. It can either make punishments more severe or increase the likelihood that punishment will be imposed or both.[3]

But the main point of this essay is to apply a model not to crime but to political variables. Let us assume that we are in a democracy with two parties: one (A) is now in power, and the other (B) is offering a different policy. The individual in Figure 1.1 prefers party B's policy to A's, as can be seen from the diagram. Furthermore, the cost of voting is very small. Thanks to the considerable advantage to be gained on the choice variable and the very slight disadvantage from the cost of action, it might be thought that the individual would be motivated to vote for party B.

Unfortunately, as Anthony Downs first pointed out, these things are not so simple. If I choose to buy a car, or for that matter steal a car, my choice is all that is necessary to carry out the act. The car will be duly bought or stolen.[4] If, on the other hand, I prefer party B and cast a vote for it, it does not follow from that act that party B will replace party A. There are millions of other people voting and their votes are as important as mine. Thus in this case I must make a probability calculation as to the likelihood that my vote will be decisive and use this to discount the improvement in the world which I would receive if the out-party B replaced the party now in, and hence the *status quo* were changed. This discounted value of the change in the government would then be set off against the cost of action. As a general rule, on the performance of the calculation it turns out that the vote itself has a negative payoff unless the individual actually gets some value out of the act of voting. If I were compelled to vote, however, as in a number of countries one is com-

---

[3] It might, of course, be sensible to increase one of these two variables and decrease the other. Thus, for example, a doubling of the risk of conviction for auto theft might be thought to justify the slash of 25 per cent in the penalty assessed. The prospective cost of the action to the criminal would still be higher than before these two actions were taken.

[4] Unless, of course, the police intervene at the actual moment of the theft.

pelled to vote, then, of course, I would always choose B. In this case, as indeed in most cases where I actually get a value from the act of voting, the cost of action is negative. I will either lose a positive pleasure by not voting or be compelled to pay a fine if the voting is compulsory and I do not vote.

But once again our model seems to be a rather clumsy way of dealing with problems which are already well developed in political theory. All I would claim for it at the moment is that it does permit the deduction of a large part of modern political theory. Thus once again we have a model which by a few changes of parameters fits a number of situations.

Let us turn to a situation to which the modern political theorists have not paid much attention. This is the problem of nondemocratic governments—in particular, despotisms. It will be immediately clear that the decision to oppose a despotic government bears much the same resemblance to a decision to vote in an election that the decision to commit a crime does to the decision to engage in economic exchange. This is not, of course, because opposition to a despotism is wicked. It is simply that society, in the person of the despot, puts a cost of some magnitude on opposition. A decision to join in a conspiracy or in a rebellion is clearly a dangerous one. The cost of this action can be very sizable. Here also, the social control variables—in the hands of the despot—are largely those of imposing punishment for unsuccessful rebellion,[5] or of making the likelihood of detection higher.

We can immediately deduce a number of propositions about revolution from our model. First, as for an individual deciding to vote, a decision to participate or not to participate in a revolution does not determine the outcome. It has only a probabilistic effect on it. Thus, the individual is not choosing between a point A and, shall we say, point B but between a certain probability of receiving A or B without his participation and another probability of receiving A or B with his participation. There will, of course, be a risk of punishment associated with the second alternative. Consideration of this fact led Dr. Thomas Ireland to propose a rather elaborate model of revolutions[6] in which the individual's likelihood of participation is a function of the number of people who have already participated. This model would be simply a special application of the very general model I

---

[5] It should be remembered that there is no punishment for successful rebellion or successful conspiracy.

[6] "The Rationale of Revolt," *Papers on Non-Market Decision Making*, III (Fall, 1967), 49–66.

have developed here. It is unnecessary to outline the further deductions that Ireland has drawn from his model, but they would be in accord with ours.

We can, however, go farther. In the first place, history indicates that despots have frequently been overthrown, but normally by some high official or group of high officials in their own regime. The romantic popular revolution is an extremely unusual event. The explanation is obvious from our model. Although the punishment for the prime minister, if he attempts rebellion, is likely to be as severe as punishment for the common man, his probability of success is vastly greater. Thus he is far more likely than the common man to find that the present discounted value of attempting to overthrow the government by a *coup d'état* is positive.

When we do find popular uprisings against a despot, whether they are successful and we call them revolutions or whether they are unsuccessful and we call them street riots or disturbances, it is usually the case that the specific incident which sets off the uprising is trivial and that there has been no carefully prepared advance planning. Again, this follows our model. A spontaneous eruption of rioting is, from the standpoint of the person participating in it, very much safer than is a conspiracy. It is far less likely that the government will be able to catch and punish him if the uprising is unsuccessful than if he enters into a conspiracy. Thus a person discontented with the government is unlikely to be motivated to join in any formal effort to overthrow it. If, however, he sees a mob coming down the street without much opposition and large enough for the chances to be good that if it gets beaten he will be able to withdraw and resume his life without the police ever knowing he participated, he may well join. Again, this is in accord with what we observe in the real world.

II. Continuous Variation

But if we look at the real world, we not only find people accepting or rejecting choices which have been presented to them by other persons or organizations; we also find people making decisions as to what choices they will present. An automobile manufacturer, for example, decides the horsepower of the engine of his car. He makes this decision in terms of the number of customers he thinks he will attract and the price he thinks he can charge them. But in making this decision he faces a continuum rather than a simple yes-no alternative. Individuals, in making offers of any kind, face the same kind of continuum, but for present purposes let us consider groups such as a manufacturer, a political party, or a despot. In Figure 1.2 I have drawn in the situation. We have some organization which, for simplicitly, let us say is attempting to sell a car to one individual. The organization has its own preference with respect to the particular choice variable as to the ideal car. Note that this is rather different from what we normally say in economics because in the actual world most people selling commodities have only relatively weak preferences as to the nature of those commodities. This is because in the

Figure 1.2. Choice on a continuum

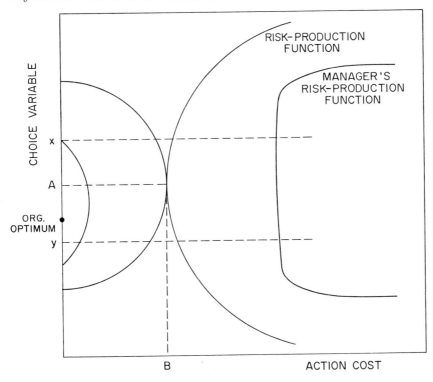

market system they are compelled to play down their own preferences. Indeed, one of the major differences between a system such as ours and a despotism is the relative unimportance of the personal preferences of the people who structure the choices in our society as opposed to similarly situated persons in a despotism.

If in making the decision with respect to the design of a car to sell to one individual the organization had perfect knowledge about that individual's preferences, it would know exactly what range of the choice variable would result in a sale to him.

Thus it would know that at any point between x and y on the choice variable the purchaser would purchase the car, and hence it would suffer no opportunity cost from a choice within this range. Outside of the area x and y the individual would not buy the car, and hence the organization would have an opportunity cost equivalent to the full potential profit on the sale of the car. The two horizontal dotted lines of x and y and the segment of vertical axis between them represent accurately the cost to the manufacturers of various choices on the choice variable axis. They would choose their optima on a particular situation represented by Figure 1.2. In practice, of course, they would not have such perfect information. It would be necessary for them to make an estimate of the likely response of the potential purchaser to each possible design of the car. Such an estimate is shown by the risk-production function in Figure 1.2. Granted the indifference curves and the risk-production function shown, the organization would choose to be at point A on the choice variable mentioned, and it would have a likelihood of an opportunity cost loss through failure to sell the unit equivalent to B.

In practice, of course, automobile companies do not adjust to individual preference orderings, but something very similar does occur. For potential changes in design or in price or in the size of their advertising budget, they anticipate differential returns in the number of units sold. They are in a sense aggregating a series of individual risk-production functions of the sort we have drawn in Figure 1.2 into a general function, which is a prediction of the number of cars that will be sold in each possible "design." Once again, they will achieve their optima in the same way and, in our particular diagram if we reinterpret the risk-production function as a representation of the number of cars to be sold at each possible design, they would choose point A and would sell B cars.[7]

It is not customary to discuss the point but an individual who is engaged in managing an automobile plant, or indeed any other industrial enterprise, faces not only possible loss of profits if his guesses as to what will sell at a given price turn out to be wrong, but he also faces a finite chance of being deprived of his position of control. If he is the manager, the board of directors may well eliminate him if things go badly enough. If he happens to own the plant or has a very

---

[7] Note that the *cost* of action is shown on the horizontal axis. Thus, *profit* and number of cars sold increase as you move to the left.

good stock position, it is clear that it will be harder for him to be removed, but as a last resort the bankruptcy court will remove him if he makes enough misjudgments. The risk of removal that management might face would have a somewhat different shape than the curve showing the total sales for cars. It will be flatter in the middle in which the total number of cars sold varies only slightly and the likelihood of either bankruptcy or stockholder rebellion is extremely slight and then much steeper at the ends, where a fall off in sales could cause great losses to the company. The owner-manager would probably have a longer flat area than would the hired manager.

In a sense, individuals deciding whether or not to buy a car are voting for or against various managements. This way of looking at the economic problem is, perhaps, not terribly helpful, since the managers of economic enterprises have a great many incentives for optimal adjustment even if they can avoid being thrown out, but it is still worth thinking about. Further, once we begin thinking about it, we realize that our model shows that a hired manager is likely to be under more pressure to adjust to the market than the owner-manager. This observation is, I think, in accord with the real world.

But once again, we appear to have developed a model which is simply a clumsy duplication of standard economic models. This is true, but I cannot regard it as a serious criticism of my essay. My objective is not to produce new economic models but to demonstrate that it is possible to obtain a general model which covers a very large number of phenomena and that this model, among other things, covers economic phenomena. Although the model is not yet fully enough developed for us to discuss such matters as monopoly and competition, it would appear fairly certain that the model would be consistent with a large part of modern economics.

Turning to noneconomic phenomena, we must first note that the model does not work very well if we think about the producer or the person who organizes the choice situation for the potential criminal as being an individual. We could use the model to determine how much money any individual would put into such things as burglar alarms, but since most decisions about crime prevention (as opposed to decisions for committing crimes) are taken politically, it is best to skip over the criminal situation and begin directly with the political model. Figure 1.2 is sufficient for our initial analysis. Let us suppose that we have some political organization, say the party in power, and that it again has preferences with respect to the choice variable, whatever it is. Its optimum is as shown on Figure 1.2. If we assume that it is running in a democratic election and that it will be removed if the majority of the voters vote against it, then the situation turns out to have very great similarity to the situation in the market. In the first place, if the political party has perfect knowledge about the response of voters and its opponent, it would know that there was a range in which it could certainly win the election bounded on either side by a range in which it would certainly lose. Once again, if the boundaries were x and y it would, on our diagram, choose its own optimum.

In practice, of course, the individual party does not have perfect information. Further, it is aware of the fact that any act it takes now will have only a limited effect on the election. It is likely that other things will happen between now and the election and the outcome of its behavior as to these is somewhat indeterminant. Therefore, once again, it has a risk-production function of the nature shown in Figure 1.2. It chooses that point where it can attain the highest indifference curve, which means it chooses point A on the diagram and runs B units of possibility of being thrown out. For the moment let us leave aside the possible existence of other parties (as we have temporarily left aside direct competition in our discussion of the market) and consider only a one-party system in which the party will either be thrown out or not, depending on the wishes of the voters. This may seem a little unrealistic, and we will shortly relax this restriction. The main point of this restriction in fact is simply to permit us to go on to discuss despotism in a fairly simple manner.

Turning then to a despotism, we again can make use of Figure 1.2 as our basic model. The despotism realizes that it can choose various social policies, and it has a policy which is optimum from its stand-point. It further realizes that there is at least a finite possibility of its overthrow. Thus, once again, it faces a risk-production function and a set of indifference curves of its own, and since we are still using Figure 1.2, it would choose policy A with the possibility, B, of being overthrown.

There is, however, a vast difference between despotism on the one hand and either the market or democratic politics on the other. This is in the shape of the risk-production function. As we pointed out before, a despotism is in a position to make opposition to itself, when the opposition is unsuccessful, extremely costly. Since individuals either voting against a democracy or joining in a rebellion can never be sure whether or not they will succeed, this ability to raise the cost of unsuccessful protest means that individuals are much more reluctant to enter into an effort to overthrow a despotism than into an effort to overthrow a democracy by voting. In consequence the risk-production function that we have specified in Figure 1.2 would be relatively close to a vertical straight line for a despotism and quite steeply curved for either a democratic party or a manager of a company. This difference is shown in Figure 1.3, where the fact that the democratic party is under much greater pressure to adjust to "the will of the masses" than is any despotism is illustrated. Note also, and I believe this is realistic, that a democratic party always runs a much higher risk of being overthrown via losing an election than does a despotism of being overthrown via either a revolution or a

Figure 1.3. Democracy and despotism

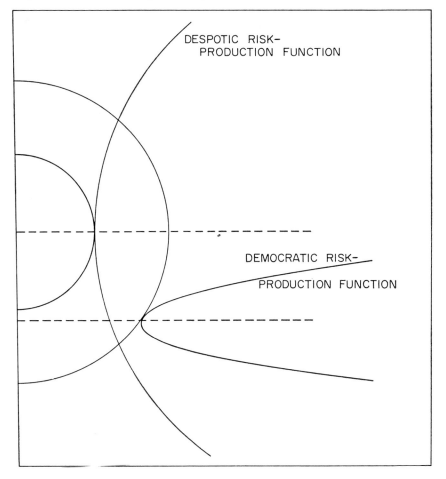

DESPOTIC RISK–
PRODUCTION FUNCTION

DEMOCRATIC RISK–

PRODUCTION FUNCTION

ACTION COST

coup d'état. We normally ignore the extreme instability of political
life in a democracy because we regard the continuance of the democratic system as being equivalent to the continuance of any given
despot in a despotism. Looked at from the standpoint of the individual politician, however, the despot is almost always more secure than
is the democratic politician.[8]

Let us now turn to the situation in which there are two possible
contenders for the favor of our collection of individuals. In this case
I must skip my usual demonstration that the model fits the market
situation because the duopoly market is at the moment an unex-
plained phenomenon. Hotelling was able to demonstrate that on any
dimension two enterprises would locate immediately adjacent to each
other, but his demonstration required the assumption that they were
charging fixed prices.[9] The moment we abandon this assumption, and
there is no reason why we should retain it, it becomes impossible to
specify the behavior of any two companies unless they enter into
some kind of conspiracy. Thus the fact that the model I am presenting here does not fit the situation is unfortunate, but it is not a great
defect. No other economic model deals with this situation efficiently
either.

Also I will not discuss the application of the model to crime, since
several groups of people committing crimes in competition with each
other seems an unlikely situation. Thus, I will proceed immediately
to democratic voting. In a way, we have been discussing democracy
with two parties when we talk about the existence of the *status quo*
and a possible change. Nevertheless, it may well be sensible to go
over the situation again without the assumption that one of the parties represents the *status quo* and there is then a proposal for change.
From the standpoint of the individual voter, there would be little
difference. He would have much the same kind of preference ordering
as that shown on Figure 1.1 and would vote for the party which was
closest to him provided that he was motivated to go out and vote.

In order to discuss party behavior under these circumstances, however, it is necessary to specify a little bit more for our model. On
Figure 1.4 I have drawn in the voters' optima. This simply is the
view of a given political party of the number of individual voters
who have their optima at any given point on the choice variable. It
is, of course, vertical to the horizontal axis, which in this case doubles

---

[8] The despot who is overthrown is, however, far more likely to find his life
ended than is the democratic politician.

[9] Harold Hotelling, "Stability and Competition," *The Economic Journal,*
XXXIX (March, 1929), 41–57.

Figure 1.4. Party politics

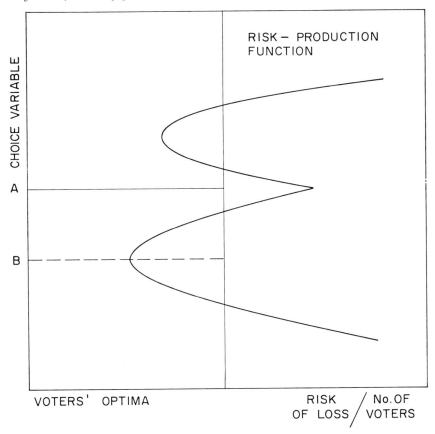

as risk and as number of voters. I have drawn the optima as a straight line because the line of reasoning which I am going to present is not in any way affected by the shape of the line and hence it seems best to use the simplest of all possible lines.[10]

Let us assume that one of the parties has already taken a position at point *A*. The other party is then attempting to determine what position it should take. In general, it will obtain all those voters whose optima are closer to its position than to point *A*. This gives it a risk-production function of the rather odd shape which I have drawn. The high risk of loss at point *A* is a bow on my part to the view that it is difficult for one party to duplicate exactly the other's

[10] Gordon Tullock, *The Politics of Bureaucracy* (Washington: Public Affairs Press, 1956), pp. 82–101.

position and still win an election. If this is not so, the curve would be a smoother one. This would make no difference in our reasoning.

Point A is somewhat above the middle of the distribution of voters, and hence the curve which shows the risk for our party is not symmetric. The party should choose, on our diagram, point B and would then be fairly certain, although not absolutely certain, of winning. Clearly, in this case, the reason that our party A is likely to win is simply that the other party made a mistake. If party B had chosen the exact middle of the spectrum of voters' preferences, it would have maximized its chance of victory. But such mistakes are unfortunately, or perhaps fortunately, common in politics.

Once again we have, in this demonstration, reproduced something that was already well known. The model is a mapping of the Hotelling-Downs mode. My point in reproducing their conclusions is simply to demonstrate the extreme generality of the model discussed here. Anyone proposing to deal solely with democracy would be well advised to use the simpler models which are available in Downs's book [11] or in my elaboration of the same concept in *Towards a Mathematics of Politics*.

III. Politics without Voting

Let us now turn to an area which is not covered in the discussion of democracy, i.e., despotism with two parties. The reader can think of himself as living in late medieval England and choosing between the Roses. Let us suppose Richmond has landed and Richard III is collecting his forces on Bosworth Field. Should the individual do nothing, support Richmond, or march to the aid of crook-back Dick? In order to discuss this problem we need a little more in the way of intellectual apparatus than we have so far presented. Still, it will be seen that basically it is the same kind of problem as those faced by any democratic party leader.

The basic difference in this matter, of course, is that the individual is likely to find a very significant cost attached to his action or inaction. The costs of going to the poll may be of some importance to the voter, but surely the costs that he will suffer in a democracy from casting his vote one way or the other are zero. Further, the cost of going to the poll is generally small enough so that a well-thought-out campaign of indoctrination can get most people to vote.

---

[11] Anthony Downs, *An Economic Theory of Democracy* (New York: Harper and Row, 1957).

The situation (shown in Figure 1.5) which confronted the individual deciding whom he would support at Bosworth Field (or indeed any person considering supporting an existing despotism or attempting to overthrow it) is more complex because of the very real costs involved. As we have pointed out before, he must make a calculation as to the likely consequences of his action. He must also make a calculation as to the likely cost to him of inaction. Thus let us suppose, as was indeed true, that the winner, whoever he was, was known to be very likely to do something extremely nasty to anyone who backed his opponent. Under these circumstances, the individual would have to determine first the likely change in the real world, i.e., the discounted value to him of the switch on the control variable to which

Figure 1.5. Choice with payments

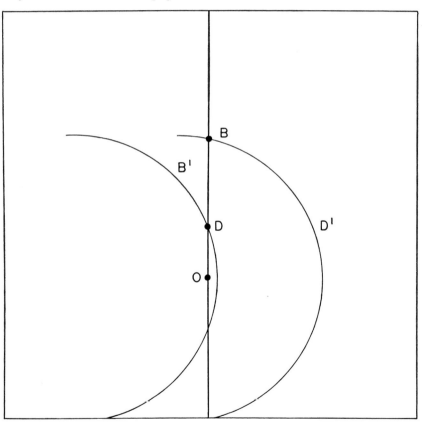

ACTION COST

his participation on the side of Richmond or Richard would lead.[12] This change would then have to be compared with the likely cost in the event of defeat for Richard. The individual might well find that this left him at point *D*, and hence that, although he preferred the Earl of Richmond to Richard III, nevertheless, he would choose to do nothing.

Note, however, that on Figure 1.5 I have drawn in a leftward extension of the original diagram. This indicates that there can be positive rewards from taking action. Let us suppose that Richard III had offered to our choosing individual a prospect of receiving some of the Lancastrian land if Richmond were beaten. This, again discounting the probable effect on the outcome which would occur from the individual's entering into the combat and the advantage of this reward in the event Richard III won and taking out the probable punishment if the Earl of Richmond won, puts the individual at point *B*. Thus he would be willing to fight for Richard even though basically he is a Lancastrian.

In practice, politics in areas of despotic government, and for that matter to a considerable extent in democratic government, does tend to turn very largely on positive rewards offered to individuals for entering into a given conspiracy or refusing to enter into a conspiracy and on the penalties for people who have made the wrong choice. In a way, in fact, the failure to make any choice at all may be a quite dangerous activity. It may be that inaction, instead of leaving the individual on the vertical line, puts him sharply to the right. This all depends on the policy of the contenders for the despotism. The problem of course is the very, very real danger involved in participating in these maneuvers, and hence the necessity for providing fairly strong incentives for people who are doing so. For most people, running such risks is not something that they will do for the public benefit. Something more than the control variable is usually necessary, and this normally takes the form of promises of advantage or threat of injury after the event. This is particularly true for the leaders.

The reader will, of course, realize that the spoils of office are also part of democratic politics. But, in democratic politics the spoils are relatively scarce. It is necessary for an individual who wishes to be President of the United States to attract more than thirty million votes. He cannot possibly directly offer favors to thirty million people on a person-by-person basis. He can, of course, do much the same

---

[12] Note that in Figure 1.5 *B* stands for boar and *D* stands for dragon. These were, of course, the symbols of Richard III and Richmond. The individual whose optimum is shown at 0 is a partisan of the House of Lancaster.

thing by offering such things as the farm program, improved welfare programs, and perhaps some cuts in taxes. But these are, generally speaking, of less value to the individual and hence would not be suitable for motivating people actually to risk their lives as is necessary in despotic politics.

Having said this, however, we must note that there have been occasions involving fairly large-scale popular support for the overthrow of a despotism, or in some cases for the support of a despotism against a potential contender. This large-scale popular support in general can be accounted for by the assumption that the two parties are far apart in their policies. As we noted before, a two-party system in a democracy tends to bring the two individual parties very close together. If one of the two potential contenders for a despotism (we may consider it the party in power) has succeeded in getting its position far enough away from the bulk of the population, then the bulk of the population may perceive the change in the policy variable which is conceivable through an overthrow of the government as large enough in and of itself to pay for running the great risks of participation in the overthrow attempt. The situation is shown in Figure 1.6. The government is at A, which is opposed by the bulk of the population. The opposition will find that, as it moves from the position of the government, the number who are willing to fight for it will begin to increase because as it moves away it offers a larger and larger implicit payment for their support. But at the same time this process is taking place, the opposition is also reducing the total number of its supporters because, as it moves away from point A, more and more people find that their optimum position is closer to point A than to that of the opposition. These two tendencies eventually lead to an optimal position which is point B in this figure. This will normally be very much farther from the position of the other party than is characteristic in a democracy, but it will still normally be as close as one can get to that position while at the same time offering a large enough change to attract people to take the risk necessary to participate in politics.

Granted this mechanism, we can readily see that the party now in power can avoid the development of a successful opposing group by simply maintaining its position close enough to the mid-point of the populace so that large groups will not wish to risk their lives to overthrow it. This normally puts only rather loose restrictions on the policy choice of the despotism. The reader will recall that we reached the same conclusion earlier when talking about a single alternative.

It should be noted in this connection that the purchase of support

Figure 1.6.   Revolt against a despotism

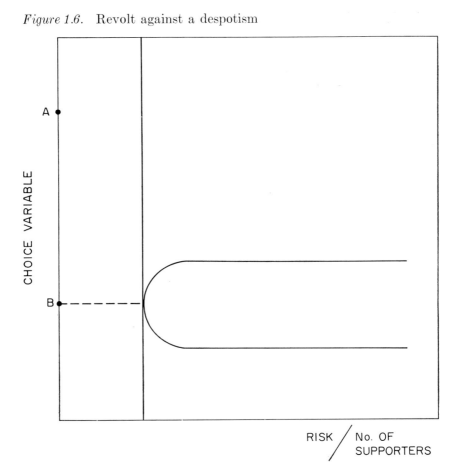

by an individual in any given conspiratorial group is a way of making certain that one is not overthrown even if one's policies are quite
unpopular. The reader will recall the Machiavelli expressed surprise
that any conspiracy ever succeeded for this reason. He argued that
the government in power should always be in a position to offer certain rewards to any conspirator who will betray the conspiracy, and
hence that no conspiracy should be successful. Conspiracies are, of
course, successful on occasion, but I think we join with Machiavelli
at being surprised at this. The possibility of such a betrayal, of
course, raises the risk of participation in the rebellion.

Having started, in this case, with the behavior of a despotism, the
organization which structures the choice, and leaving the individuals
to the end, it is now my duty to turn to the discussion of what the

citizens of a despotism should do. For this purpose we can again go back to Figure 1.1 and simply note that the cost of action is quite substantial in these cases. The individual will choose to take action if, in his view, the discounted return to him in terms of the change in the choice variable resulting from his participation in the conspiracy is greater than the discounted cost.

It should be noted that the Communists have frequently used a technique which makes this quite probable. They inflict very heavy costs, if they are successful, on people who have opposed them or who have remained neutral. A short time ago, for example, approximately 120 citizens of South Vietnam who held very minor government posts and were not sufficiently friendly to the Communists were assassinated, and approximately 250 were removed to an unknown destination. This makes the cost of action low, not because it is not dangerous to undertake action, but because it may be equally dangerous to do nothing. From the opportunity cost standpoint, the costs are low even though the absolute costs may be very sizable. Indeed, in this case it seems likely that the Communists have succeeded in making the cost of inaction greater than the cost of Communist support. Even if the Communists are eventually defeated in Vietnam, there is a very high probability that they will be able to kill any local village head who remains neutral between now and their ultimate defeat. Thus, from a standpoint of new opportunity cost, the individual, unless he feels very, very strongly anti-Communist, would be well advised publicly to adopt their cause at least. The Mafia has, of course, made use of a similar technique both in Sicily and in the United States.

So much for the two alternative cases. Turning to a situation in which there are more alternatives, however, we immediately find it impossible to use our simple two-dimensional diagram. If there are three or more people competing for customers, then they will arrange themselves not along a single line (because there will be more than two points in the choice) but along a higher dimensional figure; in the case of three people they will be at the points of a triangle. In general, in the situation of market choice, the purchaser's situation becomes easier and easier as the number of potential sellers increases, and hence there is no great difficulty in expanding the size of the model. In political choice, on the whole, the same is true. The democratic case with two-issue dimensions and three parties is discussed in my *Towards a Mathematics of Politics*, and it is clear from what we have said so far that the models used there are mappings of our models. Thus, there is no need to develop them further at this point.

That, of course, is democratic politics. If we turn to despotic politics, however, it would also seem that the conclusions of *Towards a Mathematics of Politics* would generally follow, except that the reasons for believing that the parties must seek greater differentiation and probably must offer direct payments to supporters and threaten direct punishment to their opponents are very much stronger in the case of despotic competition than in the case of competition among democratic parties.

IV. Cliques, Elites, and Parties

Thus there seems to be no particular difficulty in discussing political "competition" among almost any number of organized parties and regardless of the type of political system we are talking about. This, however, carries with it an assumption that the organized parties are monolithic, and everything we know about politics indicates that this is not so. Parties characteristically are not only fighting for control, but within each party there are a number of cliques fighting for control of the party, and there are subcliques fighting for control of cliques, and individuals trying to get control of the subcliques. In order to deal with this kind of problem, we need to complicate our model further.

Let us take a concrete example, the 1968 Democratic Convention. Consider someone who was in the camp of Vice President Hubert Humphrey during the course of the nomination campaign. In the first place, presumably he wants the Democrats to win the next election regardless of who their nominee is, although this desire may not be very strong and there are even certain circumstances in which he may hope it will lose because of the future effect on the party. Secondly, he wants Humphrey to be the nominee. His ideal situation would be Humphrey as the Democratic nominee and as the victorious candidate in the Presidential election.

Unfortunately, these two objectives are to some extent in conflict. Insofar as our Humphrey supporter makes public speeches questioning the qualifications of opponents of Humphrey in the period before the nominating convention, or indeed at the nominating convention, he decreases the likelihood that the Democrats will win in the event that Humphrey is not nominated. As we have said, it is conceivable that he does not want the Democrats to win if Humphrey is not nominated. He might feel that the nomination of Senator Eugene McCarthy followed by a McCarthy success at the polls would be a disaster either to the country or to the party, to say nothing of his own future role. A number of Republicans clearly felt this way about Senator Barry Goldwater in 1964, and in 1968 it is clear again that a number of Republicans felt this way about Governor Nelson Rockefeller. In the Democratic party a large percentage of those Democrats who backed Senators McCarthy or George McGovern have expressed themselves as feeling this way about Humphrey. The Humphrey supporters in general have not said this about McCarthy and McGovern, but there does seem to be some reason to believe that they actually feel this way, or that at least some of them do.

Nevertheless, it seems that normally it would be true that supporters of one individual candidate would still favor the success of their party even if he were not nominated. This means that we have, if we turn to the type of diagram we have been using so far for choice variables, a three-dimensional space. First, we have our policy issue dimension. Secondly, we have the probability that, in this case, Vice President Humphrey will be nominated as President, and on the third dimension the probability the Democrats will win in any case, regardless of who is nominated as President. Needless to say, for certain single-minded, ambitious politicians who are interested only in themselves, the probability that Humphrey would win the final election after having been nominated would be their sole concern. This would be the product of the second and third factors. If we assume that in most cases, however, there is no such concentration on a single objective, then we need to use three dimensions and this is, of course, impossible on a two-dimensional piece of paper.[13]

On Figure 1.7, therefore, I have drawn in only two of the three dimensions and the reader should regard it as a cross section vertical to the policy dimension. The vertical dimension shows the risk of the Democrats losing the election, and the horizontal shows the risk that Humphrey is not nominated. The risk-production function is arbitrary, since I have no idea at all what shape it will be. In my opinion Humphrey was the strongest candidate, and hence the most likely to be nominated and his nomination the most likely to ensure that the Democrats would win, but this still does not indicate very much about the shape of that curve. From the standpoint of our standard individual, presumably a zero probability of Humphrey's not being nominated and a zero probability of Democratic failure, i.e., the origin, is the optimum point. I have drawn in two indifference curves from which the reader can deduce that the particular person I have chosen is a relatively modest partisan of Humphrey, perhaps favor-

---

[13] Some draftsmen are able to produce three-dimensional diagrams, but not I.

Figure 1.7.   Choice within a party

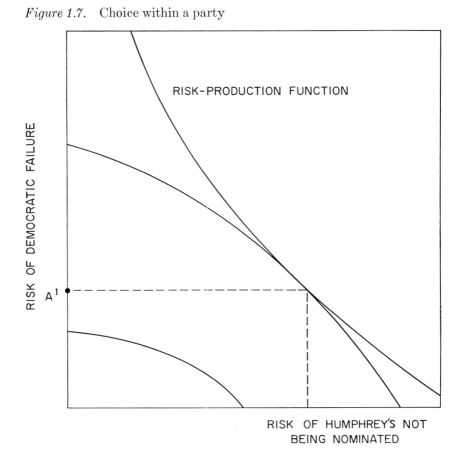

ing Humphrey only because he feels that he will maximize the possibilities of Democratic success, and he chooses a combination of action which leads to a relatively great risk that Humphrey will not be nominated and a near minimum risk that whoever is nominated will lose. That is, my particular subject would not campaign very vigorously or openly for Humphrey. He might, of course, be quite vigorous in the back room.

If the politician who is a member of the Humphrey clique felt the way many of the people who have backed McCarthy felt, then his indifference curves would be very much more steeply slanted, and he would choose to argue very strongly in favor of his candidate and against the other candidates on the ground that this increases the likelihood of his candidate's winning the nomination. The reduction in the likelihood of the Democrats' winning regardless of their candidate would be to him of relatively little importance.

We can, of course, carry our present procedure farther by looking at people who are within various cliques. Let us consider Richard Goodwin, for example. He clearly is not in the "mainstream" of the Democratic party, but in its left wing. Further, he has close and apparently extremely warm connections with the Kennedy family. He first made efforts to get Robert Kennedy to run for President. When this failed, he became one of the early backers of Senator McCarthy. It should, of course, be noted that he did not begin backing McCarthy seriously until it became clear that McCarthy was a serious threat to Johnson. Immediately upon the entrance of Kennedy into the race, Goodwin switched to the Kennedy camp. Probably that is where he felt most at home. With the death of Senator Kennedy, Goodwin switched with equal speed back into the McCarthy camp. After the convention he entered Humphrey's entourage. His ability to move into the McCarthy camp so readily after having once moved out is a tribute either to Goodwin's political abilities or to the general disorganization of the McCarthy camp.

Note that there is every reason to believe that in whatever camp he happens to be at the moment, Goodwin tries to attain a position as high as possible. Secondly, I think the evidence indicates that he chooses which particular branch of the left wing of the Democratic party he will be in primarily in terms of who he thinks will win. But my point in discussing Goodwin is not that I find him terribly interesting but that he illustrates very nicely the possibilities of the model which I have presented. As a Democrat he can be regarded as a part of a party system contesting the support of the voters. Furthermore, he has shown no signs of embarrassment when the American system changed from a two- to a three-party system. Needless to say, the switch back to a two-party system, which is highly likely in the immediate future, will equally cause him no difficulty. His own personal position, however, is entirely within the Democratic party, and he is clearly committed to its general victory. It is true that he might have been willing in 1968 to work against Democratic victory in order to improve his position within the party in the future, but basically he can be regarded as being a member of an elite, i.e., the Democratic party, which is attempting to contest with another elite for popular support. But within this elite in a sense he is again a party man. The personal followings of the Kennedy family and Senator McCarthy perform much the same function within the Democratic party as parties in the general body politic. As we have noted,

Goodwin has participated actively in this particular contest. Finally, he is willing to switch from one clique to another to improve his position. Each of these various statuses can be used as a single example of the type of model which we have presented. Further, we can produce a compound model in which each status is contained within the preceding one which will fit his total situation.

Note that in our models we can assume that a clique or a subclique has what amounts to a preference function, if it has a decision process. Further, it is quite possible to discuss situations in which, let us say, two subcliques struggle for control over one clique which in turn is attempting to influence and lead the total body politic. Such a complex situation would be simply a set of models of the sort we have described so far nesting one within another. We could deal with each particular aspect of the problem individually or we could produce a multidimensional model using the Davis-Hinich matrix model to deal with the entire problem from the standpoint of any individual within the subclique.

Nor is it necessary to confine ourselves to democracy. If we had chosen an example from a despotism, a similarly complex situation could be developed to cover the role of an individual or a clique within the despotism. Thus the model is extremely general and will cover substantially any system.

But there seems no point in continuing with further elaborations. It is clear that the model presented in this essay can be used to cover an extremely broad part of human action. With appropriately chosen parameters it will duplicate the market or duplicate those parts of democratic political theory which have been already developed. With another set of parameters, it can be used for crime, and with still another set, for a nondemocratic government. It is likely that its principal value will be in the study of nondemocratic governments and in the study of those aspects which do not, strictly speaking, fit democratic theory. In particular, it could be useful for the elucidation of the role of elites of various sorts within a democracy.

Some Decisions in the Regression Analysis of Time-Series Data

2 Bruce M. Russett
Yale University

Bruce M. Russett
Yale University

THERE are several problems in the analysis of a set of data that very much interest me. The basic substantive question is: What kinds of spending, public and private, are negatively associated, over time, with spending for the armed services? The method consists of regressing defense, as the independent variable, against a variety of others as dependent variables. We cannot *prove* causation for any resultant associations that appear, but we can at least make a plausible case for causation. Such a case is aided by selecting cases and periods where (1) the defense share of gross national product (hereafter D/GNP) is large enough to constitute a substantial resource drain on the economic and political systems and (2) there is considerable variance in both the independent and dependent variables. The United States since 1939 fits these criteria well, and I examined the data in some detail earlier.[1] The analysis, however, raised a number of methodological problems with important theoretical and substantive implications. Some of these problems are well considered in the existing methodological literature of the social sciences, especially economics, but others have been given little if any attention in the material I have examined. Hence it seems worthwhile to discuss some of them, outlining my own learning process in the course of this Odyssey through a research project.

[1] "Who Pays for Defense?" *American Political Science Review*, LXIII (June, 1969), 412–26, and *What Price Vigilance? The Burdens of National Defense* (New Haven: Yale University Press, 1970), chs. 5 and 6. This research has been supported by the Yale World Data Analysis Program, from grant no. GS–2365 from the National Science Foundation and contract no. N–0014–67–A–0097–0007 from the Advanced Research Projects Agency, monitored by the Office of Naval Research. I am grateful to Paul Berman, John D. Sullivan, and Jean Walbroeck for our discussions on these matters. No other individual or agency, of course, is responsible for errors of fact or for the opinions expressed.

I. The Unit of Analysis

The data consist of expenditure totals for various components of the GNP, such as consumption and investment (each subdivided by major categories), exports, imports, and government expenditures. Thirty annual observations over the period 1939 to 1968 are available on each variable. They appear as totals in current dollars, but cannot be used in bivariate regressions in that form. Through a combination of inflation and real productivity increases the total dollar value of the United States GNP grew by nearly a factor of ten over the period examined. Since virtually all of the components also increased sharply over the same period,[2] we would have high, and for our purposes spurious, correlations between variables measured in current dollar amounts. We need some method to take out this expansion and inflation trend effect, leaving us essentially with data on fluctuations in the shares of GNP accounted for by each of the categories. There are several possible procedures.

A. We might use data on expenditures in *constant* prices rather than in current dollars. Such data, however, are not available for some components—notably defense—and in any case would control only for inflation, not for productivity increases.

B. We might use multiple regression and partial correlations, with year and defense as two independent variables, to isolate the independent effects of each. This would take out long-term secular trends of third variables causing increases in both defense and other spending categories, for example, public expenditures generally. It would especially take out much of the inflation- and expansion-induced variation from the relationship of primary interest. Indeed, it would be even better for the latter purpose to use GNP (instead of year) and defense as the independent variables. Such a procedure is often recommended and is feasible with our data because of the effect of World War II. Since in those years military expenditures skyrocketed to a level not matched even in 1968, the two independent variables (defense and either year or GNP) are not highly correlated with each other. Thus we avoid the problem of multicollinearity, and the partials really would measure independent effects of each.

---

[2] Spending for the armed services is a partial exception to this, as the dollar amount during World War II had not quite been surpassed by 1968. Military expenditures did rise fairly steadily with a growing and inflating economy after 1946, however, and that would be sufficient to produce correlations with other expanding expenditures.

The difficulty is that, with our data, most of the variation in the dependent variables will always be accounted for by GNP (or year) rather than by defense. Yet though the variance accounted for by defense will necessarily be small, it is precisely that part of the variance in which we are substantively interested, and so we need some procedure that allows us to concentrate upon it.

C. We might regress the values of each of our expenditure variables against year or GNP (since changes in all are correlated closely with time and GNP), compute the residuals from the regression line of "expected" values, and then correlate the residuals of defense vs. time (or GNP) against those of each of the other variables vs. time (or GNP). This would take out much of the inflation- and expansion-induced variation, and hence much of the spurious correlation. Economist Frederic L. Pryor, in a book of great methodological and substantive interest to political scientists, does this with his data on the 1956–62 period.[3]

The problem here is precisely the World War II peak of defense spending. If regressed against either year or GNP for 1939–68 using the basic linear regression model, the regression line for defense would be essentially horizontal as a result. Yet if one looks only at the period since 1946, a marked upward secular trend is indeed apparent. The same would be true if one began with 1939 but omitted the World War II years. This trend would remain in the residuals to distort any regression with the dependent variables (where the trend would largely be taken out because they went down or stayed constant in World War II) and not truly keep defense and time separate. Hence the procedure deals only with secular variation and is not satisfactory where, as in these data, episodic variation in one variable is very great. Furthermore, it has been shown that the coefficient for the regression of the residuals—after taking out time or GNP—is exactly the same as would be obtained by using a multiple regression equation in the first place.[4] Therefore this procedure produces no gain in information over that in point B above.

D. We might simply divide every expenditure figure by the current value of GNP in that year, giving the proportionate share of all in-

---

[3] *Public Expenditures in Communist and Capitalist Nations* (Homewood, Ill.: Irwin, 1969).
[4] Ragnar Frisch and Frederick V. Waugh, "Partial Time Regression as Compared with Individual Trends," *Econometrica*, I (October, 1933), 387–99. For a good if very basic introduction to fitting trend lines or curves to the time-series data, see Frederick E Croxton and Dudley J. Cowden, *Applied General Statistics*, 2d ed. (Englewood Cliffs, N.J.: Prentice-Hall, 1955), p. 251 and chs. 12–16 generally.

come devoted to that category. This meets the above objections, is what I worked with in the previously cited material, and is what I will use here. But even this method has its faults. One is that ratio regressions are likely to be deceptive, producing *positive* correlations if the variation in the variable used as a denominator (here GNP) is of the same magnitude as that of the numerators (defense and various civil expenditures). This is because by using GNP in the denominator of both variables we are in part relating GNP to itself.[5] With these data, however, it is not a major problem because the variation in GNP (the range is less than from 1 to 9) is so much less than that in defense (range about 1 to 60) and less than that in most of the dependent variables (the range varies from about 1 to 7 for consumption to greater than 1 to 20). Anyway, we know that virtually all the correlations between defense and other variables, even in ratio form, are *negative*, not positive.

The second potential problem is that where we are dealing with ratios which for every given year add up to a constant, we must *expect negative* correlations among all the variables. This is relevant for some of the major categories; i.e., in the basic accounting formula

$$D/GNP + C/GNP + I/GNP + CG/GNP + X/GNP - M/GNP$$

does equal unity in every year. Thus by definition if one ratio goes up in any year some or all of the others must go down for that year, and if the relationships among the variables are truly random, one will find predominantly negative but spurious correlations.[6]

Are the negative correlations found between D/GNP and our other ratios thus spurious, since they would be expected even with random relationships among the numerators? No, because we are hypothesizing a causal relationship to be behind the correlations of defense with the others, and hence we expect *positive*, not negative, correlations *among* all the *other* ratios. That is, defense changes will force some changes in almost all of the others, so that when one goes down almost all of them will go down. And in our data that is in fact the case, since for 59 of the 66 pairwise correlations among the *dependent* variables the sign is positive. Furthermore, with random variables of this nature we might get predominantly negative correlations between defense and civil spending but would not expect the very high r^2s that

[5] For a mention of these problems see W. Allen Wallis and Harry V. Roberts, *Statistics: A New Approach* (Glencoe, Ill.: Free Press, 1956), pp. 546–56; also Edward R. Tufte, "Improving Data Analysis in Political Science," *World Politics, XXI* (July, 1969), 641–54, and the references there. It is not generally noted, however, that the difficulty depends largely on the relative variances of the denominator vs. the numerators.

[6] This point was raised in a personal communication from Michael R. Leavitt.

we often find, indicating a regular, systematic relationship between defense and *certain kinds* of other spending. Thus the focus of our attention is not on the general fact of those negative correlations, but in seeing where the correlations are strong and where relatively weak, and also substantively on the regression coefficients (slopes) and proportionate reductions suffered by the various expenditure categories.

II. The Autocorrelation Problem

The phenomenon known as autocorrelation frequently arises with time-series data. It occurs whenever the value of one observation is not independent of previous years' observations for the same variable. This is not just a problem of trend effects—that could be taken care of by one of the above methods—but remains if the *residuals* from the trend are correlated.

Autocorrelation is clearly a problem here. (1) The independent variable—defense—and several of the dependent variables respond to exogenous variables that operate over periods of several years. For example, a long-term perceived threat that requires a defense build-up will provide episodic variation and a higher than "expected" level of military spending over a number of years. So will a major war that takes several years to fight. (2) It is possible to increase expenditures, say for defense, only by some often quite limited amount from one year to another. Past procurement commitments of civilian goods and services frequently cannot be broken to free resources, and personnel and production bottlenecks will prevent a very rapid expansion in defense industry. Similarly, once defense procurement decisions are made, it may be difficult to reverse them. Hence a threat that exists only in this year may still affect levels of spending for several years to come, and for neither defense nor for the dependent variables (though probably especially for the first) is one year's observation completely independent of another's.

A check on my data showed substantial autocorrelation: virtually all of the variables indicate a probability of autocorrelation exceeding .99, using the Durbin-Watson statistic.[7] It is worse when one looks

---

[7] The basic article on autocorrelation is D. Cochrane and G. H. Orcutt, "Applications of Least Squares Regression to Relationships Containing Auto-Correlated Error Terms," *Journal of the American Statistical Association,* XLIV (1949), 32–61. See also Herman Wold, *Demand Analysis* (New York: Wiley, 1953), and J. Johnston, *Econometric Methods* (New York: McGraw-Hill, 1963), ch. 7. For the Durbin-Watson test and tables of various values of it, see J. Durbin and G. S. Watson, "Testing for Serial Correlation in Least-Squares Regression," parts 1 and 2, *Biometrika,* XXXVII (December, 1950), 409–28, and (June, 1951), 159–78.

at the *level* of D/GNP (or the proportionate level of any other variable) and less if one works only with the *changes* in level from one year to the next as the basic analytical variable (see below). But even in the latter case serious autocorrelation is present.

So what? We know that estimates of the intercept and slope of the regression equation (*a* and *b*) are unbiased by autocorrelation, and those coefficients will be primary objects of our analytical attention. Similarly, autocorrelation will not bias the r^2 (proportion of variance in one variable accounted for by another). Of course the r^2 will be high if both variables respond over the same period of years to the same exogenous influence, but we will want to know that in any case and it is not an autocorrelation problem.[8] What autocorrelation will do, however, is to produce *sampling variances* of the *estimates* of the coefficients that are unduly large, and hence autocorrelation will inflate the statistical significance of our results if we try to apply significance tests.

One response to this is simply to shrug it off as irrelevant. We certainly do not have, with these data, the "classical" conditions of sample and population, the conditions that we associate with much research in psychology and sociology, or with survey research. We would be hard put to say what the population of observations ought to be, and certainly in taking thirty consecutive years for their substantive interest we hardly have a random sample of anything. Nevertheless, significance tests are useful for gauging the strength of a relationship against the amount of random variation to be expected in a set of data. In econometrics, where the classical conditions often are no better met than here, significance tests are widely applied, and a sophisticated rationale for their use has been built up.[9] Without taking the significance levels of our findings *too* seriously, it would nevertheless be useful to refer to them.

There are other problems, in addition to sampling and autocorrelation, that work against too easy acceptance of whatever significance levels may seem to apply to our data. For one, we have deliberately selected a set of observations that not only is nonrandom but that includes years with extreme values of some variables, notably defense. The D/GNP ratio for 1944 is the highest this nation has ever experienced, and 1939 was deliberately included so as to have a figure lower than any we have seen since, or may likely ever see again. Depending on whether the extreme values are predominant in the

[8] Although it will make it dangerous to attribute any dependent relationship between the two variables.

[9] See Johnston, *op. cit.*, ch. 1, for a good example of the argument.

independent or the dependent variable, they will affect the r^2, the slope, or both. If extreme values are present in the independent variable, the r^2 will be exaggerated. For another, in some distributions the extreme values are few, and the distributions depart seriously from normality. The D/GNP distribution, for example, contains two outliers (for 1943 and 1944) which are more than three standard deviations from the mean. This departure from normality will distort, and often exaggerate, the r^2.

In this research, I simply had to face the fact of autocorrelation, and of other difficulties. Extreme values are manageable so long as they are found largely in the independent variable (as will be shown to be the case below); the effect of outliers can be controlled by transforming the variable, carefully checking the scatterplots, or, as will be done below, by repeating the analysis for periods that exclude the extreme values. But except with great complexity perhaps, not much can be done about autocorrelation. With these data, the best procedure seemed simply to apply a very strict test of statistical significance. Thus I chose a much more demanding test than I would normally use with so few observations: the significance level of .001 with a one-tailed test.[10] But with the test at such a high level, we can fairly safely assume that any results that reach that *apparent* level are worth noting and not solely the result of departures by our data from the assumptions one would like to make about them. And we should remember that the b coefficients are not affected in any way by autocorrelation.

III. Simultaneous or Lagged Relationships?

The most interesting problems, largely because they have been little discussed in the literature, deal not with de-trending or statistical significance, but with the basic hypothetical model one has about the relationship between the variables. It becomes necessary to ask, with some care and detail, what one's basic hypotheses are. The question sounds simple enough: we want to know whether the ups and downs in D/GNP are related to variations in other classes of expenditure. In the original *American Political Science Review* article I related

[10] For the b coefficients, I used the t-test from Hubert Blalock, *Social Statistics* (New York: McGraw-Hill, 1960), p. 442, and for the r^2 I adapted the table in Bruce M. Russett *et al.*, *World Handbook of Political and Social Indicators* (New Haven: Yale University Press, 1964), p. 262. Note that in the tables of this paper, only instances where *both* the r^2 and the b weights are "significant" at the .001 level are marked as significant. In fact, however, for most equations either both the r^2 and the b weights meet the test, or neither does.

annual shares of D/GNP to the annual shares of other variables, such as personal consumption, in the same year.

Yet there are plausible alternative procedures that still fit the question as loosely formulated. For one, it might be important to look for lagged effects in spending. It may, for example, take a year, or even several years, for defense demands to squeeze out other demands and be fully felt in other sectors. This might especially be true in the public sector, where governments are committed to certain spending programs, where construction may be underway and not be terminable except after a year or more, and where there may be many tenured employees who cannot readily be discharged. Accordingly I lagged the dependent variables one year behind the level of defense spending. The results, which indicated little importance for lag effects, are shown in Table 2.1.

Table 2.1. Simultaneous relationships between defense and civil spending, and relationships with a one-year lag

r^2

	Model A		Model B		Model C	
	Simul.	Lag	Simul.	Lag	Simul.	Lag
Personal cons.	.84*	.41*	.89*	.14	.39*	.28
Con. durables	.78*	.58*	.76*	.24	.95*	.25
Nondurables	.04	.00	.66*	.06	.24	.10
Services	.55*	.38*	.61*	.08	.54*	.31*
Fixed inv.	.72*	.52*	.80*	.34*	.17	.30*
Nonres. struct.	.62*	.38*	.77*	.13	.11	.19
Dur. equipment	.71*	.53*	.54*	.41*	.16	.49*
Res. structures	.60*	.45*	.13	.23	.10	.08
Exports	.67*	.25	.58*	.21	.14	.19
Imports	.19	.18	.01	.00	.02	.19
Fed. civil gov't.	.38*	.49*	.29	.13	.12	.07
S+L gov'ts.	.38*	.36*	.40*	.27	.48*	.50*

* Significant at the .001 level

The various models A, B, and C will be explained below. They represent three different ways of looking at the relation between defense and other spending, and for now their differences need not concern us. What is important is that with each we can compare the effect of a one-year lag with the regressions done for the simultaneous (same year) effect of defense. All r^2s significant at the .001 level (as explained above) are noted with an asterisk.

For neither model A nor model B does the one-year lag add appreciably to the predictive power of defense expenditures. On the contrary, for 11 of the 12 dependent variables in each model, the r^2 for the lagged relationship is lower and in fewer instances is it significant. Only with model C are the lagged relationships not consistently weaker than the simultaneous ones; there six of the 12 r^2s are higher for the lag, though even in those cases none of the lagged r^2s are very high (above .50). Yet in general the model C relationships consistently behave differently than do those of the other two models, and, as we shall see, model C is less theoretically appropriate to our understanding of the relationship between defense and civil spending.

The effect of longer lags (more than one year) might in principle have been computed, but it was apparent on inspection of the data that in general they would produce only still weaker relationships. Basically we conclude, therefore, that if changes in military expenditures are to have an effect on different types of civilian needs, the greater impact will be felt quickly rather than after a delay. Probably to the degree that lagged effects are important, they vary among specific components. For some kinds of purchases the effect may be virtually simultaneous; for others it may be felt most strongly with a few months' delay; for still others, as in the procurement of advanced weapons with long development lead times, it may be a matter of several years. If we had component data on construction, maintenance, salaries, and the like, perhaps with those further broken down by types of purchases, the lagged relationships might be clear. But with the highly aggregated categories that we have, the simultaneous relationship generally works better than anything else.[11]

Methodologically, this is just as well. For technical reasons, the use of lagged variables in a regression equation can lead to problems

[11] In fact, the closest relationship might emerge, if we had the data, in a lag between *obligations* for defense and expenditures for other goods (rather than between defense expenditures and other expenditures). It has been shown that military obligations have a sharp effect on employment in the defense industries with a lag of from several months up to a year. Similarly, in the Korean mobilization the major expansion in economic activity came at about the same time as military programs were announced and authorized, and while many of the defense orders were being placed. Most of the growth in economic activity came before the major increase in federal expenditures. See Edward Greenberg, "Employment Impacts of Defense Expenditures and Obligations," *Review of Economics and Statistics*, XLIX (May, 1967), 186–98, and Murray L. Weidenbaum, "The Economic Impact of the Government Spending Process," *Business Review*, VIII (Spring, 1961), pp. 39–40. If defense needs are thus anticipated through various fiscal and monetary mechanisms by other segments of the economy, so that by the time the military expenditures themselves go up civilian spending is already being contracted, no time lag (at least when working with annual rather than monthly data) would be appropriate.

in estimating the *coefficients* (instead of just the sampling variances of the estimates of those coefficients). This is especially likely to occur in conjunction with serious autocorrelation, which we have already acknowledged as a source of potential difficulty in our data.[12]

IV. Selecting the Observations—Which Years?

As noted above, we certainly do not have a random sample of observations, or years, from some universe of all possible years. Instead, we have deliberately selected the last three decades for analysis. That choice allows us to see the last "normal" peacetime years (1939 and perhaps 1940), the historic peak of American defense effort in 1943 and 1944, and the moderate but sustained exertions of the cold war. Yet that choice, in addition to being nonrandom, also gives us a highly skewed distribution of data points, with 26 of the observations ranging between 1 per cent and just over 13 per cent, and the other four between 31 and 42 per cent.

Even with a truly bimodal distribution, when running regressions on the entire period we would risk having most of the variance explained only by variations between the two extreme types of year (peace and cold war vs. total war), rather than by variation among those years *within* each group. This risk is greater with a skewed distribution, where the difference between a few outliers and all the rest can produce high r^2s even if there is no systematic relationship during most of the years and in "normal" circumstances. Thus we must think rather carefully: Do we particularly care about the effect of extreme values or are we more interested in the normal years? We must choose the "sample" accordingly. If the answer is that we wish to know both, or are unable to decide, then two cautionary steps are appropriate:

1) We can split the time period into several segments, running the regressions separately for each. Since for my substantive purposes I did indeed want to know both what kind of systematic relationships existed in "normal" years and how the World War II era differed from other years, I divided the observations into one segment 1939–46 and another 1946–68 (using 1946, a transition year, in both) and ran all the regressions for each subperiod separately as well as for the entire 30-year span. We will compare them carefully below.

2) The other step, always desirable under any circumstances, is to pay special attention to the scatterplots and use curvilinear regres-

[12] See Johnston, *op. cit.*, pp. 211–21. As a general reference on related problems, see Chester W. Harris, ed., *Problems in Measuring Change* (Madison: University of Wisconsin Press, 1963).

Figure 2.1. Defense expenditures as a percentage of U.S. GNP, 1939–68. Reprinted, with permission, from Bruce Russett, "Who Pays for Defense?" *American Political Science Review,* LXIII (June, 1969), 413

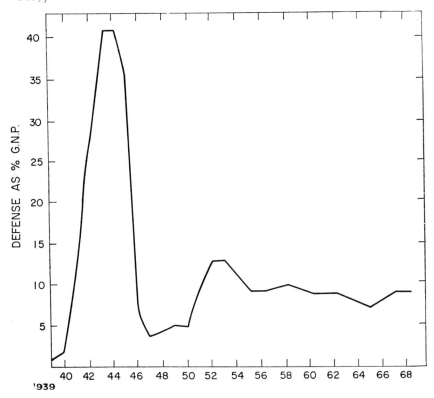

sion, as in the original analysis. That way we look behind the regression coefficient and can see whether the variance explained is a result only of differences between war and "normal" years, or whether it is produced by differences within one or both of the subperiods as well.

The presence of some extreme values in our distribution need not, however, be considered solely as an obstacle to statistical interpretation. In regression analysis extreme values can, if their effects are properly understood, strengthen our confidence in the resulting coefficients. We begin by recognizing that any nonrandom *selection* of years is likely to involve some "manipulation" of the data—whatever years we pick, the selection will affect the results in our r^2s and in our coefficients. Knowing that, we can assess what the likely effects will be and perhaps take advantage of those effects. For example, if we were to choose years so that there were very great changes in the *dependent* variables, especially with extreme values, the effect of third or "nuisance" variables would be exaggerated, and both the r^2s and the regression coefficients would be sensitive to the effects and might be very misleading. On the other hand, if there were much greater variation in the *independent* than in the dependent variable, the result could be to our benefit. The consequence would be to raise the r^2s to a level higher than would occur with less variation, but also to provide a *more accurate estimate of the slope, the b coefficient*.

Thus the fact that our defense data include both the last "peacetime" year and the great exertions of World War II means that including both those extremes will give us quite a reliable estimate of the slopes—how much of a change in the dependent variable is typically produced by a given change in defense. But the r^2s are likely to be higher than would be produced by analyzing data for shorter periods, especially for the postwar period alone. This supposition is confirmed by examining the ranges of all the variables; for defense, the independent variable, the range is approximately a factor of 30, between 1.4 per cent and 41.6 per cent. For the dependent variables, however, the range is always much narrower, at worst a factor of 10 and usually much less. So the result of deliberate choice of years with extreme values in defense can be estimated. "If there is any degree of assurance that in effect manipulations have been made primarily in terms of the independent variable, then comparisons involving slopes will be more meaningful than those using correlation coefficients." [13]

Hence we will pay special attention to the regression coefficients, for reasons other than our theoretical interest in the amount of change that only the slopes can indicate. At the same time, awareness of the effect of our "manipulation" will require us to look carefully at the several choices of years (1939–46, 1946–68, and 1939–68) to see just what the differences are. If we are looking for the effect of changes in defense, it surely makes good sense to begin with periods experiencing great changes, providing that we do not generalize too readily to the supposed effects of more moderate ups and downs.

V. In What Way Do Changes in Defense Affect Other Expenditures?

There remains an important theoretical question that has so far been ignored, and which all too often is never explicitly raised in the

[13] H. M. Blalock, *Causal Inference in Nonexperimental Research* (Chapel Hill: University of North Carolina Press, 1964), p. 126. The discussion in the two paragraphs above draws heavily on Blalock's exposition.

analysis of time-series data: What is the nature of the relationship we expect? It is not enough to hypothesize that defense and, say, consumption are related, or even enough to consider the possibility of lags. *Levels* of different kinds of spending may be related to each other, or the effects may be stronger for *changes in the levels*. There are at least three possibilities within the context of our original decision to work with expenditures as a percentage of GNP:

A. A direct relationship between *levels*, with defense affecting consumption in the form

$$\frac{C}{GNP} = a + b\left(\frac{D}{GNP}\right) + e$$

where a is the intercept, b the slope, and e an error term. This model assumes that it is a high level of defense expenditure that gets in the way of normal civilian spending; that heavy defense spending drains away resources that can be replaced for the civilian sector only after some substantial period of time. The structure of the economy is likely to be very different at high levels of defense spending than at lower ones.

B. The relationship may be one between *absolute changes* from t_0 to t_1 in the shares of the two variables, with

$$\frac{C}{GNP_1} - \frac{C}{GNP_0} = a + b\left(\frac{D}{GNP_1} - \frac{D}{GNP_0}\right) + e$$

By this view, a shift in the defense proportion from 2 to 3 per cent of the GNP will have the same effect (slope) on consumption as will a shift from 12 to 13 per cent in the defense share. The level at which the shift originates is irrelevant.

C. The relationship may be one between *proportionate changes* from t_0 to t_1 in the shares of the two variables, with

$$\frac{\dfrac{C}{GNP_1} - \dfrac{C}{GNP_0}}{\dfrac{C}{GNP_0}} = a + b\left(\frac{\dfrac{D}{GNP_1} - \dfrac{D}{GNP_0}}{\dfrac{D}{GNP_0}}\right) + e$$

This is in effect the elasticity model of economics. It says that a change in the defense share from 2 to 3 per cent of GNP will have the same proportionate effect on other variables as would an increase from 10 to 15 per cent.

Which seems more plausible? With awareness of the power of the elasticity model in explaining individual consumption behavior in economics, one might be tempted to choose it. But even in the economics of the consumption function, the pattern is less simple than might seem to be the case. Elasticities may be long or short run; an individual's consumption may be a function of his current income (à la model C) or possibly of his income in the previous period (model C with a lag), or conceivably of his anticipated income in the forthcoming period. Or, as the logic and research of men such as Keynes, Dusenberry, and Modigliani have asserted, his consumption may result from a combination of his current income and his highest previous income level. This is especially likely to be true if incomes are falling, when at least for the short run consumers may try to maintain their established expenditure patterns by drawing on savings or going into debt.[14] Thus by analogy, aggregate spending on certain categories, such as government civil purchases, might be some complicated function of a combination of current defense spending levels, absolute changes in defense spending, percentage changes in defense spending, and levels or changes of other expenditures. There is no reason why the regression equation might not have a number of independent variables each making a contribution. From the experience of economists studying consumer behavior, there is in fact reason to expect a complex relationship. We shall try a couple of simple multivariate models, but essentially, for reasons of parsimony, we shall keep to the examination of bivariate relationships. The number of possibilities even there is sufficiently large to occupy a paper of this size fully, and in any case the results of the two multivariate models we will examine are not especially encouraging.

Basically, the elasticity model (C) does not seem very appropriate to these problems, despite its usefulness in other situations. It appears that for most goods and for most industries, it is the *amount* of increased demand from the armed services, rather than the *percentage shift* in that demand, that matters more. Early in the cold war defense went up from 3.92 per cent in 1947 to 5.17 per cent in 1949; with the Vietnam war the military share rose from 7.33 per cent of GNP in 1965 to 9.23 per cent in 1967. In each case the increase was a little over 25 per cent of the base year's share, but the proportion of national resources at issue was appreciably less in the early preparedness effort. Only in the recent expansion, however (where the *share of resources being reallocated was appreciably larger*) were very serious choices forced and major strains on other programs produced.[15] Where the strains are not great, there may be a number of ways to ease them, and all of these ways may be not at all like the

----

[14] See Wold, *op. cit.*, ch. 14.

[15] One should nevertheless note that there was more slack in the economy in the late 1940's than in the mid-1960's.

choices made under great strain. Thus I would not expect the elasticity model (C) to show such regularities in the relationships between defense and other categories as do models A and B, though we shall examine the model C case to see if that is indeed true.[16]

As for a choice between A and B, the grounds are less certain. By much the same reasoning as above, I believe one would reasonably expect the level of defense spending (model A) to be more regularly associated with the level of other expenditures than would changes in defense be associated with other changes. Whereas something must always give as defense goes up, it may not be the same kind of civilian expenditure at different levels of defense spending. Thus we found that during moderate rearmament periods consumers spend less on nondurables, but during World War II their access to services and durable goods became so depleted that, lacking other outlets for their incomes, they spent quite heavily on nondurables. Even an examination of the correlation between levels of different expenditures will not identify this as a simple linear relationship, but some association will show up, to be supplemented by a careful examination of the residuals and perhaps by curvilinear regressions. Concentration merely upon changes in spending levels, however, would find nothing if it were not the amount of change but rather the share-of-the-economy base from which the change occurred that was important in determining the effect. Thus I would expect, though with less than complete confidence, that model A would be the most powerful, and that is what I used in the original analysis.

It is therefore essential to think in some detail about how the relationship between different kinds of spending is likely to work, giving attention to the particular varieties of spending (e.g., government purchases, which must be budgeted in advance, may behave quite differently than do many types of consumers' expenditures) and to the general characteristics of the economy (e.g., market or mixed economies may not distribute burdens in the same way that centrally directed ones do). On the particular questions raised in the preceding paragraphs, there is little information or even theorizing in the economic literature that I have examined, though some important suggestions are to be found. Like the economists, only rather later, students of politics are shifting from static concern with existing systems to inquiring how systems change. In the process of analyzing time series they are finding new methodological problems. The area is

---

[16] Also, we are dealing with GNP as composed additively of various components, defense and the dependent variables. For this purpose, then, models A and B, which are linear and provide automatic additivity, may be inherently superior to the elasticity model C, which is nonlinear.

important enough to merit examining our data with all three of the above models.

VI. The Choice of Years

With the two major sets of problems raised (choice of years or observations and the choice of model for searching out the relationships) we have complicated the empirical study. To keep the discussion from becoming too confusing, we will concentrate first on the selection of years problem, holding constant the choice of model (A, B, or C). We will look successively at three different tables with each

Table 2.2. Model A—relationships between levels of defense and civil spending

	1939–1968		1939–1946		1946-1968	
	r^2	coeff.	r^2	coeff.	r^2	coeff.
Personal cons.	.84*	–.420	.98*	–.500	.53*	–.643
Con. durables	.78*	–.163	.96*	–.118	.04	–.050
Nondurables	.04	–.071	.83*	–.182	.22	–.684
Services	.55*	–.187	.86*	–.199	.01	–.090
Fixed inv.	.72*	–.292	.92*	–.190	.07	–.110
Nonres. struct.	.62*	–.068	.79	–.044	.10	–.029
Dur. equip.	.71*	–.110	.84*	–.071	.18	–.099
Res. struct.	.60*	–.114	.96*	–.075	.01	–.041
Exports	.67*	–.097	.77	–.082	.42*	–.218
Imports	.19	–.025	.28	–.007	.26	–.100
Fed. civil govt.	.38*	–.048	.68	–.070	.02	–.029
S+L gov'ts.	.38*	–.128	.72	–.100	.04	–.158

* Significant at the .001 level

table limited to a single model. Within each table we will look at the r^2s and regression coefficients (slopes) for the relationship between defense and civil spending for each of three time periods (1939–68 inclusive and the World War II and postwar spans separately).

If we look first at Table 2.2 and model A only, we note that the regularity of the pattern is very striking. The r^2s are, without exception, higher in 1939–46 than over the entire 30-year span, and uniformly higher in the latter set than during the 1946–68 period alone. The mean r^2s for each of the three sets are, respectively, .81, .54, and .16. Only two r^2s for the postwar period are high enough to be statistically significant as that term is used here: those for all personal consumption and for exports. This is just as we had been led to expect, because the variation in all variables is greatest for the wartime years and least for the postwar period alone.

As Blalock indicated, however, the regression coefficients are not nearly so sensitive as are the r^2s to the selection of years. Between the 1939–68 and the 1939–46 sets, the mean difference in the coefficients is only .137, and in no consistent direction. The slope for personal consumption is the highest in each case. The difference between the coefficients for 1946–68 and each of the other sets is greater than the difference between the two sets that include the war years (as is to be expected), and in the postwar period the total consumption slope is only the second steepest, falling slightly behind that for services. If one is interested *generally* in the slopes, then one of the first two—and probably the 1939–68 set, with more data points and

Table 2.3.   Model B—relationships between changes in defense and civil spending

	1940–1968		1940–1946		1947–1968	
	r^2	coeff.	r^2	coeff.	r^2	coeff.
Personal cons.	.89*	−.461	.96*	−.462	.31	−.423
Con. durables	.76*	−.139	.92*	−.133	.48*	−.288
Nondurables	.66*	−.181	.84*	−.189	.01	−.043
Services	.61*	−.140	.85*	−.140	.55*	−.093
Fixed inv.	.80*	−.234	.93*	−.226	.54*	−.451
Nonres. struct.	.77*	−.058	.96	−.060	.00	−.005
Dur. equip.	.54*	−.082	.71	−.078	.30	−.178
Res. struct.	.13	−.095	.94*	−.087	.42*	−.269
Exports	.58*	−.108	.99*	−.112	.01	−.052
Imports	.01	−.003	.03	−.004	.04	−.026
Fed. civil gov't.	.29	−.040	.78	−.042	.01	−.022
S+L gov'ts.	.40*	−.058	.82	−.055	.10	−.066

* Significant at the .001 level

more significant coefficients—is preferable for its presumed greater "accuracy." Even so, one must still be careful. For example, only the 1946–68 set shows the *positive* relationship between defense and imports that one would usually hypothesize. As explained in the original article, many normal imports were unavailable in World War II, so the United States was unable to draw on them to meet its defense needs and thus imports were much lower than "expected."

For Table 2.3 and model B, again the World War II span [17] shows

[17] Here the World War II years are 1940 to 1946, because this model deals with the changes from one year to the next, and hence we begin with the changes between 1939 and 1940.

r^2s that are uniformly higher than the comparable ones for the entire 1940–68 span and, with only a single exception, the 1940–68 r^2s are higher than those for the postwar years only. This was expected, though it is worth noting that the average r^2 for the postwar period is higher here than for model A (the mean is .23), and four of them are significant. The regression coefficients, moreover, are virtually identical in the 1940–46 and 1940–68 periods; the mean difference is a mere .004. Even when the postwar era is compared with the other two, the mean difference is less than .090, and in every case the coefficients agree in sign.

Table 2.4. Model C—relationships between percentage changes in defense and civil spending

	1940–1968		1940–1946		1947–1968	
	r^2	coeff.	r^2	coeff.	r^2	coeff.
Personal cons.	.39*	−.043	.48	−.053	.37	−.043
Con. durables	.95*	−.105	.23	−.135	.44*	−.185
Nondurables	.24	−.026	.50	−.041	.02	−.011
Services	.54*	−.050	.62	−.053	.08	−.031
Fixed inv.	.17	−.127	.98*	−.180	.45*	−.192
Nonres. struct.	.11	−.119	.97*	−.210	.00	−.008
Dur. equip.	.16	−.089	.26	−.114	.26	−.190
Res. struct.	.10	−.282	.97*	−.444	.36	−.319
Exports	.14	−.109	.37	−.180	.00	−.022
Imports	.02	−.011	.03	−.011	.03	−.036
Fed. civil gov't.	.12	−.242	.20	−.329	.33	−.059
S+L gov'ts.	.48*	−.086	.48	−.073	.12	−.070

* Significant at the .001 level

Model C in Table 2.4 shows much the same sort of picture with the r^2s as did the first two and need not be discussed in detail. Substantial similarity between the coefficients in 1940–68 and 1940–46 again shows up, though not as dramatically as in model B. The 1947–68 coefficients are not too different except that three coefficients (for nonresidential structures, exports, and imports) are positive instead of negative. But since their r^2s in 1947–68 are trivial this is of no concern.

VII. Comparing the Models

We shall now compare the differences produced by the three analytical models, holding the years constant. The data are the same as those of the last three tables, so we shall not present them again. The reader should look first at Tables 2.2 and 2.3, comparing the appropriate columns in each. We have little basis to choose between models A and B with regard to r^2s. For the entire 30-year time span, the mean difference in r^2s is less than .17 in a set of high r^2 values, and there is no consistent direction of the difference; that is, neither model shows consistently higher r^2s than does the other. Only two r^2s, those for nondurables and residential structures, are *very* different. Comparing the wartime years in each, there is extremely little variation between one model and the other. Among r^2s that typically run at .85, the mean difference is less than .09, again with no consistent difference in direction. For the 1944–68 comparison the difference is greater (a mean difference of .27), with much lower r^2s to start with, though even here there is no consistent direction for that difference from one method to the other.

Likewise the coefficients in the two models are very much alike for the two time cuts that include the World War II years (mean difference of .037 in 1939–68 and but .026 in the 1939–46 wartime years alone). Nevertheless the 1947–68 coefficients are *quite* different, if in no consistent manner, between the two models. There indeed it does make a difference which one applies. This conclusion should not be stressed too heavily, however, in light of the warning that if years are chosen where the variation in the dependent variable is not great, the regression coefficients will be unstable and of doubtful value for generalization.

We shall conclude this section by comparing only Tables 2.2 and 2.4 for models A and C, since A and B are not very different and the reader can compare B with C for himself. For the entire 30-year span, the r^2s in C are usually (75 per cent of the time) *much* lower than in A (the mean difference is roughly .26); the same is true comparing 1939–46 in the two tables. The 1946–68 r^2s are quite different from one model to the other, but there is no consistency in the direction: model C is just as likely as A to show the higher r^2 for a given variable. Yet the typical r^2 in each table is so low (the mean for model A in these years is but .16, and that for model C only .20) that the differences seem to have little import. The coefficients vary greatly, with two enormous differences (.600 and more) when the postwar years are matched.

Generally, one has to conclude that model C does not show high correlations between spending for the armed services and spending for civilian needs. The exceptions are for three items of investment or quasi-investment in 1946–68: total fixed investment, residential structures, and consumers' durables. For these variables model C shows a moderately strong relationship with defense, while model A indicates essentially no association.[18] In the postwar period where the level of defense spending has never approached its World War II heights, the model (A) that emphasized differences in spending levels suggests that investment has been undamaged by rising defense needs and not indulged during military cutbacks; the elasticity model nevertheless shows some interesting linkages where its perspective is taken. But with this exception, the elasticity model does not predict well to the intended dependent variable. It is not the appropriate model for these data and these substantive interests. To say it differently, if one's theoretical interest is in the elasticity model, defense proves to be a poor predictive variable. But with either of the other two models, defense is a powerful predictor, and the model one selects does not make too much difference in the conclusions.

Finally, on the basis of economists' experience with consumption functions we suggested that civil spending might be some complex function of defense and other expenditures, perhaps incorporating both levels and changes. The number of possible equations is virtually infinite, and the number of plausible ones is very large; here we can look at only two. They will attempt to improve on the relationships found for model A and model B respectively, incorporating both defense levels and changes in those levels in equations as follows:

$$\frac{C}{GNP} = a + b_1\left(\frac{D}{GNP_1}\right) + b_2\left(\frac{D}{GNP_1} - \frac{D}{GNP_0}\right) + e$$

and

$$\frac{C}{GNP_1} - \frac{C}{GNP_0} = a + b_1\left(\frac{D}{GNP_1}\right) + b_2\left(\frac{D}{GNP_1} - \frac{D}{GNP_0}\right) + e$$

Table 2.5 compares the results of these multiple regression equations with the two-variable equations of models A and B for the entire 30-year period.

As is readily apparent, the improvement obtained by adding another independent variable is very slight—in all but 4 of the 24 cases an increment of .10 or less to the r^2s. The only major exception is for residential structures in model B, where adding a term for the previous level of defense spending helped substantially. It is of course true that in most instances we started with very high r^2s, so perhaps too much improvement could not have been expected. Possibly there are other circumstances where some combination of levels and changes would prove to have greater power.

---

[18] Incidentally, and here the reader should look also at Table 2.3, in these instances model C and model B are in close agreement.

Table 2.5. Comparison of models A and B with two-independent variable equations, 1939–68

	r^2 Model A	Model A plus D change as an independent variable	r^2 Model B	Model B plus D level as an independent variable
Personal cons.	.84*	.88*	.89*	.91*
Con. durables	.78*	.85*	.76*	.78*
Nondurables	.04	.10	.66*	.79*
Services	.55*	.55*	.61*	.68*
Fixed inv.	.72*	.82*	.80*	.81*
Nonres. struct.	.62*	.73*	.77*	.77*
Dur. equip.	.71*	.81*	.54*	.54*
Res. struct.	.60*	.66*	.13	.68*
Exports	.67*	.77*	.58*	.59*
Imports	.19	.24	.01	.01
Fed. civil gov't.	.38*	.51*	.29	.32*
S+L gov'ts.	.38*	.41*	.40*	.45*

* Significant at the .001 level

VIII. A Summation

Several points can be made briefly:

A. The choice of years makes a very substantial difference in the strength of the apparent relationship (r^2s) between defense and the dependent variables. As we had been led to expect, the regression coefficients are much more stable than the r^2s. If one is unable to find usable data for observations that will show great variation in the independent variable, he may nevertheless hold the regression co-efficients with some confidence and may feel that his r^2s understate the relationship that would become apparent if only he had data showing more variation. This is especially true if his interest is in the kind of relationship described by model B. As for the conclusions of the original article, *the significant coefficients there, based on the entire 30-year period, can be generalized with good accuracy to the wartime and postwar eras separately.*

B. Models A and B differ little in their substantive conclusions, except perhaps for the 1946–68 period. Both of them show a strong effect of defense upon many kinds of civil spending, so in this sense the choice of model A for the original article did not importantly bias its conclusions. Model C, however, generally shows little systematic defense-civil interaction except for some interesting relationships in the postwar period. Unless one has a particular interest in the elasticity model, it may often best be discarded. Complex multiple regression equations may sometimes be helpful, but two tried here were not.

C. Overall, the choice of years and the choice of model does make enough difference so that the analyst must think carefully about what is appropriate to his questions and his data. If unable to make a choice in the abstract, he should not hesitate to look at his data in several different ways and report the differences.

D. One further substantive point should not be lost. There is some evidence that in the 1939–46 World War II period, when defense began from a very low level and the total government budget (defense and civil, all levels of government) was lower in 1939 than it has ever been in the last two decades (under 15 per cent as compared with 20 per cent or more), B may be a better model for discovering the impact of defense on *public civil* spending. Generally, it may be a better model where the variation is great and where there are extreme values for the independent variable. In model A for the wartime years, the r^2s for federal civil purchases and for state and local government expenditures were, respectively, .68 and .72; in model B each was ten points higher. Politically determined expenditures may be more sensitive to great changes in the level of defense spending than to the actual height of those levels. Governments resist sharp changes in their total budgets, and in the short run are likely to cut other expenditures in order to make room for new military needs without too greatly inflating total budgets. Over time, however, public perceptions of what total budget is appropriate are likely to change, so that a high level of military demand, if it was also high in the preceding year or two, may still be compatible with heavy public spending for civilian functions.

These efforts have enabled us to say something more about the relation between defense and other kinds of spending in the American economy, and they have largely strengthened our confidence in the earlier findings on this topic. Nevertheless, they only scratch the surface of possible study. Detailed scrutiny of different expenditures at different levels is needed; categories should be disaggregated further; and specific questions (How does all-out war differ from rearmament, or from times of limited war? How mirrorlike are relationships when defense is on the upswing to those in times of military cutbacks?) must be examined within the general framework of this approach.

Spatial Models for the Analysis of Roll-Call Data

3 Duncan MacRae, Jr.
University of Chicago

LEGISLATIVE votes are being studied increasingly to throw light on problems and subjects such as those of social and political cleavage, the structure and functions of political parties, constituency relations, the conditions of political careers, and the distribution of power. They have been used by historians and sociologists as well as political scientists. International bodies, courts, and political parties may be studied by techniques similar to those used for national, state, and local legislatures in various countries at various historical periods.[1] Because of this extensive application of a particular class of techniques of analysis, it is important that the foundations of these techniques be firmly established. This paper will therefore be devoted to problems that seem formal in nature and perhaps distant from the politics of particular legislatures, but which have nevertheless arisen from the study of legislative politics in France and the United States and from critical evaluation of the rapidly growing literature in related fields.

Many of the arguments and models we shall advance are not completely new to the literature, being known in psychometrics or mathematics. They are, however, insufficiently available to political scientists; some have been used in the political science literature in ways that are open to criticism; and they require particular modifications for the study of roll-call data. We attempt therefore to give some of the necessary bibliography, to select those aspects of it that are most necessary for roll-call analysis, and to indicate the modifications of standard techniques that are required for this subject matter.

We begin by defining the problem in formal terms and limiting the range of the models we shall consider. First, the roll-call data are

---

[1] Illustrative references are given in D. MacRae, Jr., *Issues and Parties in Legislative Voting: Methods of Statistical Analysis* (New York: Harper & Row, 1970), ch. 1.

considered to be dichotomous—yea and nay. We bypass the problems of treating either absences, abstentions, or the various other forms of votes that exist in some bodies.[2] For congressional votes in particular, absences will be treated as missing data; while they provide valuable information for some problems, we shall not treat them.

We shall be concerned here with *spatial* models and primarily with the two-dimensional case. The model of one-dimensional Guttman scaling has been used extensively in roll-call analysis and has proved fruitful. But especially in the study of legislatures in which partisanship is an important variable, an extension of this model to more than one dimension is highly desirable.[3] The most difficult step seems to be that from one to two dimensions; and because this step involves so many problems, which can be illustrated by diagrams on paper, we shall consider only the one- and two-dimensional cases rather than extensions to spaces of higher dimensionality.

A spatial model is one in which the parameters are quantitative spatial coordinates or relations between them. Such a model, for our present purpose, involves points and distances between them, or lines and distances of points from them. By focusing attention on models of this sort, we set aside those other models whose parameters are classifications of legislators or roll calls. These latter models, which may indeed be useful for roll-call data, include cluster analysis of roll calls or legislators; multiple scalogram analysis; and latent structure analysis, insofar as its parameters involve latent classes. We also set aside the cumulative or Guttman scale model, at least in the version that gives rise only to a ranked set of legislator categories and roll-call cutting points.

Our aim in using any model of this sort is to simplify the voluminous data that roll calls provide, approximating them by models expressed in terms of a smaller number of parameters. The relations between these parameters and the roll-call votes should be consistent with our knowledge of legislative decision processes; and if the model is to be fruitful, the parameters should also have meaningful relations to variables other than those derived from roll calls, such as constituency relations and career patterns.

All the models with which we shall be concerned include parameters for both roll calls and legislators, and all characterize legislators by points in a space. The models differ, however, in their characterization of roll calls. The earliest model of this type, developed for the

---

[2] For example, "did not take part in the vote" (French National Assembly); concurring opinion (U.S. Supreme Court).

[3] See MacRae, *Issues and Parties,* pt. II.

general treatment of multicategory items by Guttman, assigned a separate numerical value to each of the two responses on a dichotomous question or roll call.[4] This model typically gave rise to a multiplicity of dimensions for a single Guttman scale and does not lend itself well to the study of the interrelation of multiple issue dimensions corresponding to distinct issues, or of issues and partisanship.

Another difficulty with this model is that it apparently lacks parsimony. To specify the parameters for any roll call, in a space of r dimensions $2r$ coordinates must be given. But the partition of legislator points into two subsets requires only the definition of a straight cutting line or hyperplane, which can be defined by only r parameters. In the plane, if the model specifies that a legislator's reproduced vote favors that alternative whose point is closest to his own point, then only the perpendicular bisector of the line segment joining the yea and nay points need be specified. Since this line is the same for an infinite set of pairs of points, and since the line alone determines the adequacy of reproduction of the data by the parameters of the model, the two-point model includes unnecessary parameters.

There remain several models that are parsimonious in this sense. One which has not yet been applied retains the two-point model for each roll call, but studies only those roll calls that involve a choice between new legislation and the previously existing state of affairs. For these, the existing state of affairs can be regarded as a constant point shared by all roll calls, e.g., the origin.[5] In this way the two-

---

[4] See Louis Guttman, "The Quantification of a Class of Attributes," in Paul Horst *et al.*, *The Prediction of Personal Adjustment* (New York: Social Science Research Council, 1941); Guttman, "The Principal Components of Scale Analysis," ch. 9 in Samuel A. Stouffer *et al.*, *Measurement and Prediction* (Princeton: Princeton Univ. Press, 1950). Related methods have been developed by Chikio Hayashi, for example, in "Multidimensional Quantification, with the Applications to Analysis of Social Phenomena," *Annals of the Institute of Statistical Mathematics* (Tokyo), V, no. 2 (1954), 122–43. They have been applied to survey data in Ichiro Miyake, "A Comparison of the Components of Electoral Decision in the Varying Kinds of Election," *Zinbun: Memoire of the Research Institute for Humanistic Studies* (Kyoto University), no. 8 (1966), 1–26; to American election statistics and international trade flows in Michitoshi Takabatake, "Application of 'Quantification' Scaling to Socio-political Data" (Rikkyo University, Tokyo), 1967, mimeographed. They are also described in Hayward R. Alker, "Statistics and Politics: The Need for Causal Data Analysis," in Seymour Martin Lipset (ed.), *Politics and the Social Sciences* (New York: Oxford, 1969), pp. 280–82, 289–95, and 308–13.

[5] The alternative "that the existing state of affairs be unchanged" is singled out for attention in Duncan Black, *The Theory of Committees and Elections* (Cambridge: Cambridge Univ. Press, 1958), p. 4 and *passim;* and in D. MacRae, Jr., *Dimensions of Congressional Voting,* University of California Publications in Sociology and Social Institutons, I, no. 3 (1958), 371–72.

point model can be retained without requiring two new points for each roll call. A second alternative is to generate the partition of legislators corresponding to a given roll call not by a hyperplane but by a hypersphere such that those legislators whose points are near the roll-call point favor it, while those farther away oppose it. This latter type of model has been referred to by Weisberg as *proximity* scaling [6] rather than *dominance* (cumulative) scaling. A model of this type used by Lingoes characterizes each legislator by a point and reproduces the votes of legislators according to whether the distance of a legislator point from a roll-call point is greater or less than a specified minimum.[7]

In models of this sort, several methods have been used to estimate the parameters for legislators and roll calls. One is to compute numerical indexes of association or similarity between pairs of roll calls or pairs of legislators; to compute spatial positions for roll calls or legislators from these indexes; and then to compute the parameters or coordinates for the legislators or roll-calls—whichever were omitted in the earlier part of the analysis.[8] A second method, used in latent structure analysis, is to consider relations of higher order than pairwise ones between the roll calls or legislators.[9] A third method, used by Lingoes, is to solve simultaneously by an iterative procedure for both roll-call and legislator parameters.[10] Models of this sort need to be compared with respect to several criteria—for example, their validity, parsimony, mathematical justification, and computability. These comparisons may be made in several ways. First, the models and methods of solution may be applied to real legislative data. Although this approach is obviously of the first importance, we shall not be concerned with it here.[11] Second, they may be compared by means of

[6] Herbert F. Weisberg, "Dimensional Analysis of Legislative Roll Calls" (Ph.D. diss., University of Michigan, 1968).

[7] James C. Lingoes, "A General Nonparametric Model for Representing Objects and Attributes in a Joint Metric Space," paper presented at the International Symposium on the Use of Computers in Archaeology, Marseilles, France, April, 1969.

[8] Once a set of numbers for roll calls (e.g.) have been computed, by whatever means, a corresponding set of numbers for legislators can be found such that in conjunction the two sets fit the original data in a least-squares sense. See MacRae, *Issues and Parties,* ch. 7. This operation can also be carried out for the Guttman-type models cited in note 4 above. The alternation and repetition of this process would eventually lead to Guttman's solution (see *Measurement and Prediction,* ch. 9).

[9] Paul F. Lazarsfeld and Neil W. Henry, *Latent Structure Analysis* (Boston: Houghton Mifflin, 1968).

[10] Lingoes, *op. cit.*

[11] See MacRae, *Issues and Parties,* for numerous examples using both real and artificial data.

artificial data having known properties, the criterion being the extent to which relevant properties are reproduced by the computation of parameters.[12] Third, the properties of various models and procedures may be investigated by logical or mathematical analysis. We shall be concerned here with the second and third of these approaches.

An Artificial Two-Dimensional Cumulative Scale

Conventional cumulative scaling has proved useful in roll-call analysis, but it is possible that many sets of roll calls, while failing to fit this model in one dimension, might fit an extension of it to two or more dimensions. No simple computational procedures exist, however, for identifying two-dimensional cumulative scales.[13] One method that is frequently used to generate spatial parameters in multiple dimensions, however, is factor analysis. This method can be tested on artificial data and the results compared for various coefficients of association. A second method that also gives rise to spatial coordinates is nonmetric multidimensional scaling, for which we shall also present results on the same set of artificial data.

The artificial data in question were generated from the diagram shown in Figure 3.1.[14] In this diagram, thirty ("legislator") points were arranged in an equally spaced rectangular array, and twenty-six cutting lines were drawn among them. These cutting lines consisted of five sets of parallel lines; each gave rise to a partition of the legislator points and could be treated as a "roll call" by considering responses to the upper right as positive, those to the lower left as negative.

We first illustrate with these data an atypical variant of factor analysis. The logic of this approach derives from that of the one-dimensional cumulative scale: in a perfect scale pattern, any pair of items (roll calls) will give rise to a fourfold table with one empty cell. The presence of such a cell, and the degree of departure from it, can be measured by computing Yule's Q for each pair of roll calls;

---

[12] Cattell has designated such sets of artificial data as "plasmodes." See Raymond B. Cattell and Joseph Jaspers, "A General Plasmode (No. 30–10–5–2) for Factor Analytic Exercises and Research," *Multivariate Behavioral Research Monographs*, no. 67–3 (Austin, Tex.: Society of Multivariate Experimental Psychology, 1967).

[13] An accurate solution for ranked responses—very difficult to use in practice for large numbers of items—is that of multidimensional unfolding. See Clyde H. Coombs, *A Theory of Data* (New York: Wiley, 1964), ch. 7.

[14] The following results of factoring the Q-matrix for artificial data are also presented in MacRae, *Issues and Parties*, chs. 5 and 7.

Figure 3.1. Thirty artificial points with twenty-six cutting lines

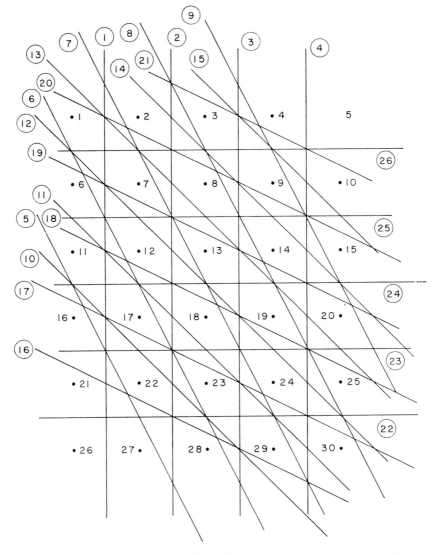

where the cells of the fourfold table contain numbers of legislators that are respectively, *a*, *b*, *c*, and *d*, the coefficient is

$$Q = \frac{ad - bc}{ad + bc}$$

A matrix of values of this coefficient between all possible pairs of roll calls may be searched for clusters of roll calls that constitute cumulative scales to a given degree of approximation, set by the threshold value of Q required for clustering.[15]

But because a perfect scale would be expressed by a submatrix in which all Q's were unity (with proper choice of polarity), factor analysis of the Q-matrix for a perfect scale would yield a single factor with all roll calls having loadings of unity. Thus by extension we consider factoring the Q-matrix to look for scales in more than one dimension, even though this matrix fails to satisfy some of the conventional mathematical conditions for factor analysis.[16] We compute eigenvectors of the Q-matrix as in principal component analysis, and then compute corresponding numbers ("factor scores") for the legislators.[17]

These computations for the Q-matrix based on the data generated by Figure 3.1 gave as the first three eigenvalues 23.1, 5.0, and 0.8, indicating a good (but not perfect) approximation to the underlying two-dimensional space. The factor loadings for the 26 "roll calls," shown in Figure 3.2, indicate that those lines that were parallel in Figure 3.1 correspond to points that lie near one another in the factor-loading diagram. The fundamental equations of factor analysis express approximate data values in terms of factor loadings and factor scores. They represent an inner product of two vectors, corresponding to factor loadings and factor scores respectively. But each of these same equations could correspond to the projections of factor-score points on a line defined by the factor loadings, this line being perpendicular to the corresponding cutting line or hyperplane. For this reason there is a close correspondence between the conventional factor-analytic model and our model of points and cutting lines.[18] Whether we should expect the locations of the points to correspond exactly to sets of parallel lines in Figure 3.1 is questionable, since the artificial "roll calls" that we have analyzed could have been produced by various configurations of points and lines, including some in which the lines were not strictly parallel.

Figure 3.3 shows the corresponding factor scores for the "legislators," computed according to a slight modification of the conventional matrix equation for factor scores. They reproduce the relative positions of the thirty points in Figure 3.1 quite well, if we consider that the "roll call" data generated by Figure 3.1 and used in the factor

---

[15] *Ibid.*, ch. 3.   [16] *Ibid.*, ch. 5.   [17] *Ibid.*, chs. 7, 8.

[18] For the equations of factor analysis, see Harry H. Harman, *Modern Factor Analysis,* 2d ed. (Chicago: University of Chicago Press, 1967), p. 15; for the correspondence with cutting lines, see MacRae, *Issues and Parties,* pp. 264–66.

Figure 3.2. Factor loadings for artificial data from Q-matrix (first two eigenvectors). Types of points correspond to sets of parallel lines

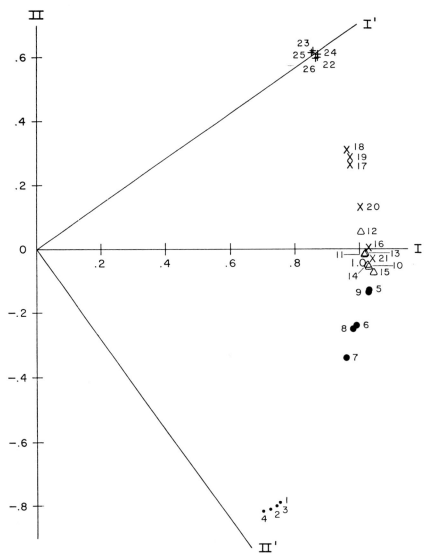

analysis are unaffected by rotation, or by a transformation of the original space that carries rectangles into parallelograms.

These results from factoring the Q-matrix are far superior to those from the conventional factoring of a matrix of ϕ-coefficients (Pearson

Figure 3.3. Factor scores for artificial data from Q-matrix (computed as $F = XA(A'A)^{-1}$, where X is data matrix with column means removed)

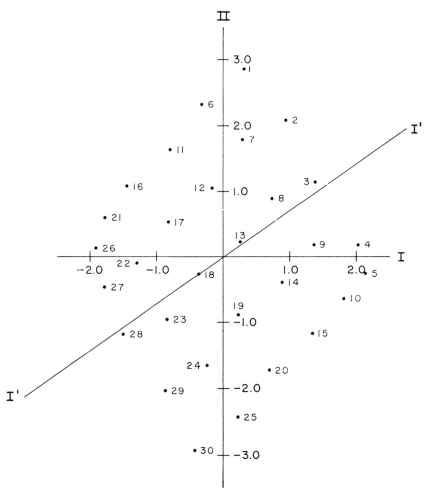

r's for fourfold tables), as Figures 3.4 and 3.5 show. Neither the parallel lines nor the configuration of points is recovered at all. Even the two-dimensional character of the space, approximately revealed by the eigenvalues in the Q-matrix analysis, disappears in the factoring of the ϕ-matrix; the first three eigenvalues were 11.5, 3.4, and 3.3 respectively.

Another method that yields interesting results for these artificial

Figure 3.4. Factor loadings for artificial data from ϕ-matrix (first two eigenvectors)

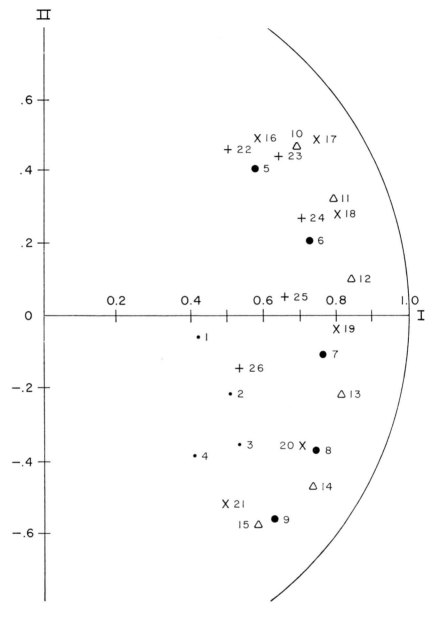

Figure 3.5. Factor scores for artificial data from ϕ-matrix (computed as $F = XA(A'A)^{-1}$, where X is data matrix with column means removed)

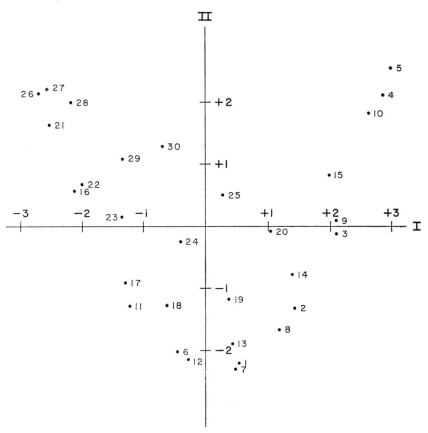

data is the Guttman-Lingoes Smallest Space Analysis.[19] This method begins with a set of pairwise coefficients of similarity or distance between elements (roll calls or legislators) and converts them

[19] Louis Guttman, "A Generalized Nonmetric Technique for Finding the Smallest Coordinate Space for a Configuration of Points," *Psychometrika*, XXXIII (December, 1968), 469–506. I am indebted to Professor James C. Lingoes for applying this method to these artificial data. An additional application and numerous references are given in Lingoes, *op. cit.* A related method is presented in J. B. Kruskal, "Multidimensional Scaling by Optimizing Goodness of Fit to a Nonmetric Hypothesis," *Psychometrika*, XXIX (March, 1964), 1–27; and "Nonmetric Multidimensional Scaling: A Numerical Method," *ibid.*, XXIX (June, 1964), 115–29.

to a ranking of the $n(n-1)/2$ coefficients. Only this ranking is used in the subsequent analysis, which finds by successive approximation a set of spatial coordinates for the n points that optimally reproduces the initial ranking. Lingoes applied this method to our artificial data, first for the legislator points and then for roll-call points. In the former case, the "distance" between two legislators was taken to be the proportion of all "roll calls" on which the pair had different responses; in the second, the "distance" between two roll calls was taken as the proportion of all legislators who voted differently on the two roll calls.

The results of these two Smallest Space Analyses are shown in Figure 3.6. The upper part of the figure shows that this method reproduced the positions of the legislator points in very much the same way as did the factor scores from the Q-matrix. In the lower part of the figure, the roll-call points are arranged so that their horizontal coordinate corresponds roughly to their "difficulty" or proportion of positive responses, while their vertical coordinate corresponds to the slope of the corresponding set of parallel lines.

This nonmetric approach appears promising, but it is difficult to establish the conditions under which it will produce unique solutions, without a supporting mathematical theory.[20] Extensive trials will of course throw light on the strengths and potentialities of nonmetric techniques as well as factor analysis, but if some comparable model were available that provided determinate metric solutions for the placement of points and lines from data of this type, it would at least be a useful and fixed standard of comparison. For this reason we turn to an attempt at formulation and solution of an explicit metric model for cumulative scales. This was, of course, the problem that Guttman initially considered, but we now wish to locate legislator points and cutting lines (or their one-dimensional equivalent) without the embarrassment of "difficulty factors" or of higher-order principal components from a perfect scale.

---

[20] A critical analysis of multidimensional approaches of this type is presented in Harold J. Spaeth and Scott B. Guthery, "The Use and Utility of the Monotone Criterion in Multidimensional Scaling," *Multivariate Behavioral Research,* IV (October, 1969), 501–15. An explicit solution treating these distances as cardinal numbers could also be attempted by the method described in Gale Young and A. S. Householder, "Discussion of a Set of Points in Terms of Their Mutual Distances," *Psychometrika,* III (March, 1938), 19–22, or the similar treatment in Walter Kristof, "Die Beziehungen zwischen mehrdimensionaler Skalierung und Faktorenanalyse," *Psychologische Beiträge,* VII, no. 3 (1963), 387–96. However, distances of this sort based on a diagram such as Figure 3.1 fail to yield an exact two-dimensional solution.

Figure 3.6. Analyses of artificial data by Guttman-Lingoes Smallest
Space Analysis (SSA)

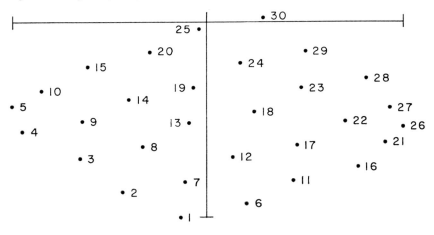

A. Two-dimensional configuration of points based on
interpoint "distances"

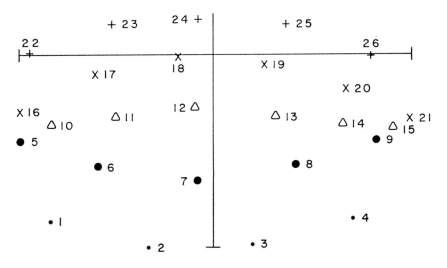

B. Two-dimensional configuration of lines based on
inter-line "distances"

A Least-Cubes Metric Model for Cumulative Scales

In search of a determinate metric solution, we therefore explore this possibility for a simple cumulative scale. In a sense this might seem a step backward, as the ranking aspect of cumulative scales has often been seen as a desirable parsimony in a model that did not justify cardinal measurement. But in the formulation of a determinate multi-dimensional model, this is a necessary preliminary step. We wish therefore to obtain an explicit metric solution for the positions of respondents (legislators) and items in such scales.

We thus wish to specify an explicit maximization criterion akin to those used by Lingoes and Kruskal. This cannot, however, be an error count or similar parameter such as "reproducibility"; such criteria, whatever their virtues, do not give unique solutions to the problem we have set. In a one-dimensional cumulative scale, for example, the goodness of fit of a solution, measured in such terms, is invariant under monotonic transformations. We are thus led to a criterion function that measures distances of points from lines. Such a criterion might be similar to that used for the discriminant function, but as we shall see, it cannot be precisely the same. We shall refer to "cutting lines" (the two-dimensional case), and then restrict the argument to cutting points, in one dimension.

Our problem, unlike that of the discriminant function, is to find locations of both points *and* cutting lines, given a data matrix. The problem of the discriminant function is to find the *slopes* of cutting lines (or hyperplanes), given the points and given the columns (roll calls or responses on dichotomous items) of the data matrix. But if we can find only the slopes of lines, and not their distances from the origin, we cannot locate the points precisely. The discriminant function defines a line (perpendicular to the cutting line) such that the projections of the points on it are optimally separated in relation to their over-all (pooled) dispersion. We thus maximize

$$\frac{(\bar{x}_{i+} - \bar{x}_{i-})^2}{\underset{+,-}{\Sigma} x_i{}^2},$$

where x_i = location of *i*th respondent (with over-all mean assumed to be zero), as projected on the line perpendicular to the cutting line, whose slope is to be found;

 $\bar{x}_{i+}$ = mean position of all respondents with + responses on item *i*, on this line;

 $\bar{x}_{i-}$ = mean position of all respondents with − responses on item *i*, on this line.

If we knew the points, we could determine the slope of the cutting line and then its distance from the origin, by moving the line perpendicular to itself to a position of maximum reproducibility or an optimum value of some other criterion function. But if the points have to be located as well and we do not know the precise location of the lines, the problem is not solvable. Extreme cutting points are needed to locate extreme respondents. The desired criterion function must therefore depend on the distances of the points from the lines and not simply on the distance of the two means from one another.

Let us now restrict our attention to the one-dimensional case and introduce the further notation,

$$y_j = \text{location of cutting point for } j\text{th item};$$

then a diagram of legislator points, responses, and cutting points would be of the following type:

With the aid of this notation, we may consider the properties of various possible criterion functions. A little experimentation should convince the reader that neither $(x_i - y_j)$ itself, nor its square, can be summed to produce a criterion function whose maximization will produce a determinate solution to our problem.

However, one function that does produce determinate solutions is a sum of *cubes* of individual distances; this criterion function may be defined as

$$(1) \quad S = \sum_i \sum_j (1/n_{-i}n_{-j})(x_i - y_j)^3 \atop \text{(minus signs)}$$
$$- \sum_i \sum_j (1/n_{+i}n_{+j})(x_i - y_j)^3 \atop \text{(plus signs)}$$

where $n_{-j} = $ the number of respondents who answer $(-)$ on item j,
$n_{+j} = $ the number of respondents who answer $(+)$ on item j.

We now set the two partials with respect to x_i and y_j equal to zero. For the y_j this gives:

$$(2) \quad \frac{\partial S}{\partial y_j} = (-3/n_{-j}) \sum_{i=j-} \frac{(x_i - y_j)^2}{n_{-i}} + (3/n_{+j}) \sum_{i=j+} \frac{(x_i - y_j)^2}{n_{+i}}$$

where $(i = j-)$ denotes respondents i who answer $(-)$ on item j,
$(i = j+)$ denotes respondents i who answer $(+)$ on item j.

Setting (2) equal to zero, we get for each nonunanimous roll call or column in the data matrix,

$$(3) \qquad (1/n_{-j}) \sum_{i=j-} \frac{(x_i - y_j)}{n_{-i}} = (1/n_{+j}) \sum_{i=j+} \frac{(x_i - y_j)^2}{n_{+i}}.$$

Thus the (weighted) average squared distance of y_j from the x_i's corresponding to $+$ responses on item j, is the same as the average for the x_i's corresponding to $-$ responses.

For the x_i the corresponding result, for each legislator, or row in the data matrix with both $(+)$ and $(-)$ responses, is:

$$(4) \qquad \frac{\partial S}{\partial x_i} = (3/n_{-i}) \sum_{j=i-} \frac{(x_i - y_j)^2}{n_{-j}} - (3/n_{+i}) \sum_{j=i+} \frac{(x_i - y_j)^2}{n_{+j}}.$$

Setting (4) equal to zero, we obtain

$$(5) \qquad (1/n_{-i}) \sum_{j=i-} \frac{(x_i - y_j)^2}{n_{-j}} = (1/n_{+i}) \sum_{j=i+} \frac{(x_i - y_j)}{n_{+j}}.$$

We shall illustrate the solution of the system of equations (3) and (5) for several elementary examples. In these examples, it will be seen that we have as many equations as there are nonunanimous rows plus nonunanimous columns in the data matrix.

EXAMPLE I

Consider the first case of one cutting point and two legislators. We designate the data matrix as

$$M = \begin{bmatrix} +1 \\ -1 \end{bmatrix}.$$

For this data matrix, equation (5) has no meaning and equation (3) becomes

$$(6) \qquad (x_1 - y)^2 = (x_2 - y)^2,$$

leading to two solutions: $x_1 = x_2$ (a "degenerate" solution which we need to reject using signs of $x - y$ differences); and $x_1 - y = y - x_2$, a solution in which the two legislator points are equidistant from y. Clearly the zero and scale factor can be set at our convenience and they do not affect the adequacy of the solution.

EXAMPLE II

The second case has two cutting points and three legislators, forming a perfect scale.

$$M = \begin{bmatrix} +1 & +1 \\ +1 & -1 \\ -1 & -1 \end{bmatrix}.$$

In this case we get three equations, two for columns and one for row 2:

(7) $j = 1$: $(1/2)(x_3 - y_1)^2 = (1/2)[(1/2)(x_1 - y_1)^2 + (x_2 - y_1)^2]$

(8) $j = 2$: $(1/2)[(x_2 - y_2) + (1/2)(x_3 - y_2)^2] = (1/2)(x_1 - y_2)^2$

(9) $i = 2$: $(x_2 - y_2)^2 = (x_2 - y_1)^2.$

Note that the equations could correspond to matrices other than M; for example, the + and − symbols could be interchanged in the entire matrix, or only in the second row. This multiplicity of possible matrices may explain the existence of several solutions, among which we must choose. Criteria for this choice need to be added in further development of the model.

As before, we have two more unknowns than equations, and we must fix these by setting the zero and scale factor of the $x - y$ dimension. The solution can be simplified by an assumption of symmetry, i.e., $x_2 = 0$. In this case, $y_2 = \pm y_1$ from (9). If we choose the solution $y_2 = -y_1$, then (7) and (8) become identical if we also let $x_1 = -x_3$. If we then let $y_1 = -1$, the only remaining unknown is the distance of x_3 from the origin, measured in units of $y_1 = -1$. The equation that must be solved can be found by substitution in either (7) or (8):

(10) $(1/2)(x_3 + 1)^2 = (1/4)[(-x_3 + 1)^2 + 2].$

Solving,

$$2(x_3^2 + 2x_3 + 1) = (x_3^2 - 2x_3 + 1) + 2$$

or

$$x_3^2 + 6x_3 - 1 = 0,$$

leading to the solutions, $x_3 = .16$ (rejected), and $x_3 = -6.16$.

It might have been expected that the five parameters, for legislators and roll calls, would be equally spaced along the horizontal axis. The inequality of spacing that we find is apparently a consequence of the least-cubes criterion.

EXAMPLE III

Next consider a perfect-scale data matrix with three items and four legislators.

$$M = \begin{bmatrix} +1 & +1 & +1 \\ +1 & +1 & -1 \\ +1 & -1 & -1 \\ -1 & -1 & -1 \end{bmatrix}.$$

Equations (3), for the columns, become:

(11) $j = 1$: $(1/3)(x_4 - y_1)^2 = (1/3)[(1/3)(x_1 - y_1)^2$
$$+ (1/2)(x_2 - y_1)^2 + (x_3 - y_1)^2]$$

(12) $j = 2$: $(1/2)(x_3 - y_2)^2 + (1/3)(x_4 - y_2)^2 = (1/3)(x_1 - y_2)^2$
$$+ (1/2)(x_2 - y_2)^2$$

(13) $j = 3$: $(1/3)[(x_2 - y_3)^2 + (1/2)(x_3 - y_3)^2$
$$+ (1/3)(x_4 - y_3)^2] = (1/3)(x_1 - y_3)^2.$$

Equations (5), for the rows, become:

(14) $i = 2$: $(1/3)(x_2 - y_3)^2 = (1/2)[(1/3)(x_2 - y_1)^2$
$$+ (1/2)(x_2 - y_2)^2]$$

(15) $i = 3$: $(1/2)[(1/2)(x_3 - y_2)^2 + (1/3)(x_3 - y_3)^2]$
$$= (1/3)(x_3 - y_1)^2.$$

If we continue to assume symmetrical solutions, we let $y_2 = 0$, $x_3 = -1$, $x_2 = +1$, $y_1 = -y_3$, and $x_1 = -x_4$. Under these assumptions (14) and (15) become identical and assume the form $(\frac{1}{3})(1 - y_3)^2 = (\frac{1}{6})(1 + y_3)^2 + (\frac{1}{4})$, leading to the solutions $y_3 = 6.08$ and $-.08$. We reject the second as unreasonable and solve (11) for x_4. Substitution yields

$$x_4 = -12.16 \pm \sqrt{187.21}.$$

We reject the solution with the positive sign as unreasonable (again, more specific criteria are desirable), and the other is then

$$x_4 = -25.84.$$

```
—|——————————————————————————|———|-|-|———|——————————————————|—
  x₄                          y₁  x₃ y₂ x₂  y₃                 x₁
```

The solution of these simple examples demonstrates the possibility of an explicit metric solution for some cumulative scales, giving rise to values for both roll calls and legislators—a solution that is completely described in one dimension without higher components. However, numerous problems remain before the least-cubes model can be used on empirical data. Procedures for matrices containing errors must be devised, and approximations will be necessary for the case with more equations than needed to determine a solution. We must avoid poor solutions due to unclear signs in squared terms. Finally, an extension to two or more dimensions, which would provide the basic justification of such a model, must be devised. Efforts in this direction so far have revealed that the two-dimensional problem is far more complex than the examples just presented, but it is hoped that eventually it can be solved.

In formulating this least-cubes model, we have sought explicit solutions for very simple sets of data. An alternative approach to establishing theoretical foundations for spatial models of this type, however, might involve analysis of limiting cases in which points and cutting lines were very numerous and dense. The exploration of both these approaches may be necessary before a sound basis for these models and procedures can be established.

Compound Paths
in Political Analysis

4 Donald E. Stokes
University of Michigan

Donald E. Stokes
University of Michigan

THE need for simultaneous equation methods in the interpretation of multivariate systems is especially evident when the investigator wishes to explore the relationship of variables which are only indirectly linked.* The need to explore such indirect ties was in fact a principal motive for the development of "path analysis," a species of simultaneous equation methods which evolved in population genetics a generation ago and which has attracted wide attention in the social sciences more recently.[1] Although the analysis of indirect or "compound" causal paths is less emphasized in social science discussions, the estimation of compound paths is in some respects the most distinctive feature of path analysis, one which can give insight into the structure of many political systems. I shall argue this point by examining an elementary but nontrivial application of these methods to political research, mentioning at the end several problems which must be solved if such methods are to give worthwhile results across a broad range of studies.

---

* Much of the illustrative material of this paper is drawn from research undertaken collaboratively with Warren Miller, to whom my debts are very large. I should also acknowledge my indebtedness to Gudmund Iversen, David Karns, Thomas Mann, and Arthur Miller.

[1] The methods of path analysis were developed by Sewall Wright and set out by him in a series of papers. See in particular "Correlation and Causation," *Journal of Agricultural Research,* XX (January, 1921), 557–85; "The Method of Path Coefficients," *Annals of Mathematical Statistics,* V (September, 1935), 161–215; and "The Interpretation of Multivariate Systems," in Oscar Kempthorne, Theodore A. Bancroft, John W. Gowen, and Jay L. Lush (eds.), *Statistics and Measurement in Biology* (Ames, Iowa: Iowa University Press, 1954), pp. 11–33. Lucid discussions of path analysis in social research have been given by several recent writers. See in particular Otis Dudley Duncan, "Path Analysis: Sociological Examples," *American Journal of Sociology,* LXXII (July, 1966), 1–16. An excellent discussion of the use of recursive and nonrecursive simultaneous equation models in political analysis is Hayward R. Alker, Jr., "Causal Inference and Political Analysis," in Joseph L. Bernd (ed.), *Mathematical Applications in Political Science, II* (Dallas, Texas: Southern Methodist University Press, 1966), 7–43.

The transfer of the methods of path analysis from the biological to the social sciences is an interesting piece of intellectual history. This was a case of parallel methodological development in fairly distant fields, especially population genetics and econometrics, with the likeness imposed by a common mathematical structure going almost unnoticed for some years. When this likeness was seen, both bodies of method could be drawn upon to solve the analytical problems for which simultaneous equation methods are appropriate. To emphasize this essential unity I shall derive here certain of the results of path analysis by utilizing structural equations and restrictions on disturbances which would be familiar to the econometrician.

My substantive example is taken from a study of the relationship of American congressmen to their constituencies. Some years ago Warren Miller and I gathered from more than a hundred congressional districts interviews of members and constituents which might help us to understand better the structure of the influence which the mass of the people may exert on their elected representatives. This research posed very clearly the need for a method of discerning the importance of indirect or compound paths of political influence, and I shall draw on certain of our published findings to illustrate the help that path analysis can give. The statistical quantities I shall cite should be regarded merely as illustrative, however, since the subsequent analysis has evolved in several major respects.[2]

A Model of Constituency Influence

A brief sketch of the design of this work may make clear why we chose the model I shall examine. This research sought to place constituencies along three dimensions of conflict in American politics: the role of the federal government in social and economic welfare, the degree of American involvement abroad, and protection by the national government of the rights of Negroes. I shall be concerned here

---

[2] The findings given here were reported in Warren E. Miller and Donald E. Stokes, "Constituency Influence in Congress," *American Political Science Review,* LVII (March, 1963), 45–56, and later, as corrected for the attenuation due to the sampling unreliability of our constituency measures, in Angus Campbell, Philip E. Converse, Warren E. Miller, and Donald E. Stokes, *Elections and the Political Order* (New York. John Wiley, 1966), 351–72. Our subsequent analysis has examined roll-call behavior from the 86th more than from the 85th Congress, utilizing a somewhat refined scaling technique and simultaneous equation models which depart in certain respects from the recursive one I shall discuss here. For these reasons the results set out below should be seen as illustrative. A full report of this work, including a detailed discussion of our measures, appears in Warren E. Miller and Donald E. Stokes, *The Structure of Representation* (Englewood Cliffs, N.J.: Prentice-Hall, forthcoming).

exclusively with the last, the dimension of civil rights. By questioning our samples of constituents about the issues which gave meaning to this dimension and by forming the mean of the positions taken by respondents from the same constituency, we sought to measure the degree of support found within each of our constituencies for federal intervention to protect the rights of blacks.

It was of interest, first of all, to see how closely the opinion of the constituency matched the behavior of the Representative. We consulted for this purpose the roll-call votes which had been cast on civil rights questions by those who represented our sample constituencies. Across the hundred-odd districts the match between constituency opinion and roll-call behavior was quite close, the product moment correlation exceeding +0.6.

Yet this statistical value provided no more than the beginning of the investigation. What we sought primarily were the *means* by which the constituency might influence its Representative. There are at least two quite different ways in which the Member's behavior may be linked to his constituency's views. The first of these involves the constituency's choosing a Representative whose policy inclinations are such that his record in Congress is likely to match his constituents' views. This pathway of influence can be seen as formed out of two connected steps: *first,* the constituency chooses a Member whose attitudes match its own and, *second,* these attitudes are then expressed by the Member's votes in the House:

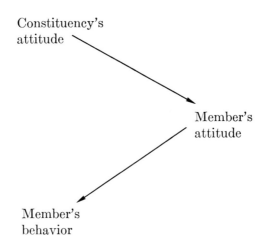

Constituency's
attitude

Member's
attitude

Member's
behavior

A second and quite different means by which the constituency may influence its representative is for the Member to mold his actions in Congress to his view of constituency opinion. This pathway of influence can also be seen as formed from two connected steps: *first*, the Member correctly perceives the constituency's views and, *second*, these perceptions guide his behavior in the House, presumably in many cases for the difference it may make when his political fortunes are again at the mercy of his electorate:

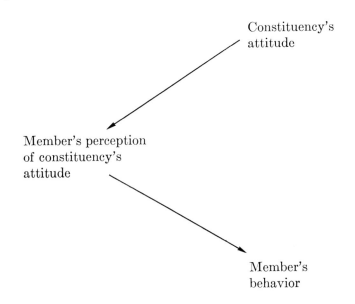

An added complexity is lent these relationships by the fact that the two intervening terms in these paths may influence each other. We would not expect the Member's own opinions to be wholly insulated from those he imputes to the constituency. Each might indeed influence the other: the Member may tend to see the constituency in his own image, but he may also embrace the constituency's views as his own. For the moment, however, I shall admit only the latter of these possibilities. I shall suppose that the Member may bring his own views into line with the views he perceives in those on whom his career in Congress ultimately depends.

These relationships suggest a simple but illuminating model of constituency influence. Let us denote by X_1 the constituency's attitude, by X_2 the Member's perception of that attitude, by X_3 the Member's own policy beliefs, and by X_4 his behavior in the House. It will be useful also to represent explicitly the role of residual influences arising outside the model itself. Let us denote by R_u, R_v, and R_w the parts of the Member's perception, attitude, and behavior respectively which are *not* determined by the measured variables of the system.

With this much notation we may exhibit the model diagrammatically as follows:

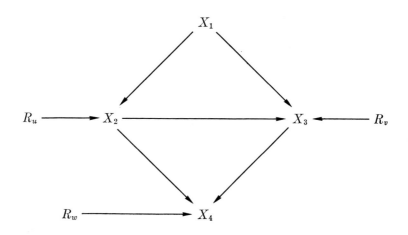

This sketch makes explicit a main aspect of the model, the absence of reciprocal causation or feedback. The single-headed arrows indicate that we assume causation moves only one way between any two variates. More generally, the impossibility of starting at any given point in the diagram and tracing a sequence of arrows that leads back to the same point makes clear the hierarchical arrangement of variables. Under the assumptions we have introduced, this is a "recursive" model.

Such a diagram can help the investigator to clarify his thoughts, and this is warrant enough for a heuristic of this sort. I will presently suggest a physical analogue which can help us visualize certain of the properties of such a system. Moreover, Wright has shown that this sort of diagram can provide the basis of the detailed calculations of path analysis. His algorithm must be one of the most interesting examples of graphic reasoning in modern science.

But in certain respects a diagram of this sort leaves the mathematical form of the model only partially specified. We shall need to write down a set of equations giving the model's structure and certain restrictions on the residual terms before we may proceed to estimate its parameters. The model includes three "endogenous" variables, that is, variables which are partially determined within the system. We shall need a structural equation for each.

Let us begin with X_2, the endogenous variable measuring the Representative's perception of his constituency's views, and write the structural equation

(1) $$X_2 = p_{21}X_1 + p_{2u}R_u,$$

indicating that X_2 results partially from the independent variable X_1 and partially from influences outside the model represented by the unmeasured residual R_u.

Several things should be noticed about the form of this equation. To begin with, it is linear in its parameters and its variables. Whether a linear specification is appropriate is of course a question that must be settled anew for each inquiry. It will frequently accord fairly well with the structure of a multivariate system, and the investigator can at times avail himself or various transformations to enhance the linearity of the relationships among his variables.

Secondly, equation (1) lacks the constant or "intercept" term that is found in a linear equation in general form. Such a term has been deleted by scoring each variable with zero mean. In the case of R_u this is done by assumption: in common with most models of this sort, this one incorporates the assumption that the mean or expectation of R_u vanishes; that is, that $E(R_u) = 0$. The variables X_1 and X_2 will have zero mean if we score each in "standard form" with zero mean and unit variance or standard deviation. Indeed, we may greatly simplify the mathematics involved in deriving estimates of the model's parameters by measuring each variable in terms of standard deviations about its respective mean. For all i, $E(X_i) = 0$ under such a scoring. In addition, for any i and j, $E(X_iX_j) = r_{ij}$ under such a scoring; that is, the covariance of any two variables will be equal to their product moment correlation. By extension, for all i, $E(X_iX_i) = E(X_i^2) = 1$.

The usefulness of these elementary properties of the mean and variance and covariance of variables in standard form will be clear below. But using standardized variables to simplify our algebra by no means implies that the investigator need always do his calculations or interpret his results in terms of such variables. In some cases, including the one I have chosen for illustrative purposes, sample standard deviations are the most meaningful units which the investigator can give his measures. But, in other cases, he is able to scale his variables in terms of other units which have a clear substantive meaning. When this is true, he may want to interpret his results in terms of nonstandardized variables, even if he has done his calculations in terms of standardized ones.[3]

I shall follow the convention of arbitrarily regarding the unmeasured factors as also having unit variance; that is, of assuming in the case of equation (1) that $E(R_u{}^2) = 1$. The virtue of this convention is that it yields a coefficient, in this case p_{2u}, which may be compared directly with the coefficients of the measured variables to assess the relative contribution of the residual factor to the total determination of a given endogenous variable. This is conventional in path analysis, but not in econometrics, where $p_{2u}R_u$ would be replaced by a single term, such as e_2 or u_2.

Much more critical is what we assume about the relationship of these residual disturbances to the independent variables. We shall assume that the residual term of each equation is uncorrelated with the independent variables appearing in the same equation. Therefore, we assume in the case of the structural equation for X_2 that the correlation of R_u and X_1 vanishes:

$$(2) \qquad r_{1u} = E(X_1 R_u) = 0.$$

A great deal depends on the truth of these restrictions on the disturbances, as will be clear below. In some cases it will be possible to make

[3] I shall not examine here in detail the question of when the investigator will want to use standardized and when nonstandardized coefficients. A judicious reappraisal of this issue is given by Sewall Wright, "Path Coefficients and Path Regressions: Alternative or Complementary Concepts?" *Biometrics,* XVI (June, 1960), 189–202. The virtues of treating variables in nonstandard form and working with "path regressions" rather than "path correlations" are discussed in John W. Tukey, "Causation, Regression, and Path Analysis," in Oscar Kempthorne *et al.* (eds.), *Statistics and Mathematics in Biology* (Ames, Iowa: Iowa State College Press, 1954), 35–66. Tukey's argument is applied to social and political research in Hubert Blalock, "Causal Inferences, Closed Populations, and Measures of Association," *American Political Science Review,* LI (March, 1967), 130–36. Blalock's illustrative use of the very research I have discussed here is somewhat puzzling, to say the least, since the values of nonstandardized coefficients would in this case be prey to wholly arbitrary choices of scale factors. Indeed, it is difficult to see how it would be possible to interpret the values of these coefficients without taking into account the variances of the several measures incorporated in our model. More generally, the claim that nonstandardized coefficients always give more fundamental information and are, in particular, more suitable for comparative inquiry seems to me quite false. There are cases, as Blalock suggests, in which the differences in the variances of empirical measures are irrelevant to the general propositions with which the investigator is concerned. When this is true, nonstandardized coefficients are to be preferred. But there are also cases, including many comparative studies, in which these differences are highly relevant to the investigator's general propositions. When this is true, standardized coefficients must be preferred. A more extended discussion of this point is set out in Miller and Stokes, *The Structure of Representation.*

a limited test of the validity of these assumptions, as will also be clear. But the investigator will often have nothing better to go on than his intuitive understanding of his research problem in saying whether such an assumption is reasonable. If this position seems a trifle naked, we may note that this simply makes explicit an assumption that is required by various analytical techniques. Such an assumption is typically required when single-equation regression methods are used to estimate some underlying structure, rather than merely to summarize an observed relationship for purposes of description or prediction. And such an assumption is no less essential when causal inferences are made from bivariate or multivariate contingency tables, as they frequently are.

We may write the structural equation for the second endogenous variate, the Congressman's own policy inclinations, as follows

$$(3) \qquad X_3 = p_{31}X_1 + p_{32}X_2 + p_{3v}R_v$$

to indicate that these inclinations are partially determined by the independent variables X_1 and X_2 and partially by the disturbances summarized in R_v. We shall again assume that the disturbance term is uncorrelated with each of the independent variables which appear in the structural equation for X_3; that is, that

$$(4) \qquad E(X_1R_v) = E(X_2R_v) = 0.$$

The structural equation for the last of the endogenous variables, the Member's behavior in the House,

$$(5) \qquad X_4 = p_{42}X_2 + p_{43}X_3 + p_{4w}R_w,$$

indicates that this behavior is partially determined by the Member's perception of the constituency and his own policy inclinations and partially by the influences outside the model summarized in R_w. The fact that X_1 nowhere appears in this equation makes explicit our assumption that the links between the constituency's attitude and the Member's behavior are indirect. We shall once again assume that the residual term is uncorrelated with each of the independent variables which appear in the structural equation for X_4; that is, that

$$(6) \qquad E(X_2R_w) = E(X_3R_w) = 0.$$

These assumptions about the relationship of R_w to X_2 and X_3 carry the important added implication that R_w must be uncorrelated with X_1 as well, since X_2 and X_3 are partially built up of X_1. Indeed, a convenient general property of recursive systems is that disturbances which are independent of variates at a given level must also be independent of all variates which are "earlier" in the system.

How may we connect the parameters of this model with empirical data? It is something of a paradox that the two writers who did most to introduce simultaneous equation methods to social and political research did not at first propose estimating the parameters of such a model. This is paradoxical in the case of Herbert Simon because his thinking was stimulated by an econometrics literature in which this sort of estimation had come to occupy a central place. It is equally paradoxical in the case of Hubert Blalock, since his later work has shown a strong interest in the information which these parameters contain.[4]

Simon was intent on finding a means of telling when the correlation observed between two variables is an artifact of their common dependence on a third variable. He saw that their correlation would be spurious if and only if the parameter expressing a causal dependence of one on the other were to vanish. When the variables are in standard form, the value of this parameter is given by a certain ratio of the simple correlations among the three. This ratio would vanish if and only if its numerator vanished; hence Simon was able to specify a relation among the zero order correlations appearing in the numerator which must be satisfied if the correlation is spurious. But nothing in this test required the calculation of the parameter's value. The investigator need only see if the necessary relation obtained among his simple correlations.

Blalock extended Simon's method beyond the three-variable case. Nonetheless, the original emphasis on testing for zero values remained. The algorithms which Blalock put into the hands of a growing company of research workers examined the correlations of a system of variables to see which were spurious. In diagrammatic terms, Blalock wanted to see which arrows might be deleted from a model, and those who employed his algorithms became preoccupied with arrow dropping.

---

[4] Simon's seminal paper dealt with the problem of spurious correlation in the three-variable case. See "Spurious Correlation: A Causal Interpretation," *Journal of the American Statistical Association*, XLIX (September, 1954), 467–79, reprinted in Simon's *Models of Man* (New York: John Wiley, 1957). Blalock's generalization of Simon's method was summarized in his influential volume, *Causal Inferences in Nonexperimental Research* (Chapel Hill, N.C.: University of North Carolina Press, 1961). But Blalock's later work has addressed itself much more directly to the estimation of parameters. See especially *Theory Construction: From Verbal to Mathematical Formulations* (Englewood Cliffs, N.J.: Prentice-Hall, 1969). For a comment on the puzzling inattention to problems of estimation in Simon's and Blalock's early work, see Raymond Boudon, "A Method of Linear Causal Analysis: Dependence Analysis," *American Sociological Review*, XXX (June, 1965), 365–74.

This sort of test failed to yield the additional information that could be obtained by estimating the parameters of a model. If one of these were found to vanish, the investigator could draw the same conclusions he would have reached by the Simon-Blalock technique. Indeed, in one important respect he would be on surer ground: since the estimators of these parameters have known sampling distributions, he could more reliably say when a near-vanishing value might be ignored. But the gain in information would be far more important in cases in which the parameters did not vanish. Indeed, the investigator who wishes to trace certain indirect or compound paths of a multivariate system must necessarily inspect the nonvanishing parameters of his structural equations. In the econometrician's phrase, he must estimate the model.

Estimating the Elementary Path Coefficients

An extensive and elegant literature, much of it due to the econometricians, deals with such problems of estimation. I shall draw only very sparingly on their techniques here. It will be useful, however, to follow in outline form how the estimation of such a model might proceed. In the case of a recursive model with independent disturbances such as that I have chosen for illustrative purposes, the optimal estimation procedure is equivalent to ordinary least-squares regression. I shall trace this procedure in a way which foreshadows the use of "instrumental" variables when the investigator must deal with a nonrecursive model. The method involves our multiplying through each structural equation of the model by the independent variables which appear there, taking expectations, and finding that the resulting terms are all either observed correlations or quantities assumed to vanish under the restrictions we have placed on the error terms. Let us see how this stratagem unfolds.

We begin with the structural equation for X_2, given by equation (1) above. If we multiply this equation through by X_1, the only independent variable which appears there, we obtain

$$X_1 X_2 = X_1(p_{21}X_1 + p_{2u}R_u)$$

(7)

$$= p_{21}X_1{}^2 + p_{2u}X_1 R_u.$$

If (7) expresses an equality, we shall still have an equality if we take the mean or expectation of each side of this equation across all observations:

$$E(X_1X_2) = E(p_{21}X_1{}^2 + p_{2u}X_1R_u)$$

(8)

$$= p_{21}E(X_1{}^2) + p_{2u}E(X_1R_u).$$

We now avail ourselves of several convenient facts about the terms of this equation. Since our variables are in standard form, $E(X_1X_2) = r_{12}$ and $E(X_1{}^2) = 1$. And since we have assumed, in equation (2) above, that R_u is uncorrelated with X_1, we may delete the term $p_{2u}E(X_1R_u)$ as having a vanishing value. Hence, equation (8) reduces to

(9) $p_{21} = r_{12},$

and we have derived an estimate of the parameter p_{21} in terms of the observed correlation of X_1 with X_2. Indeed, in this case correlation is equal to "causation," as Simon noted. Since the correlation and regression coefficients have identical values in the bivariate case when each variable is in standard form, an estimate of p_{21} is equally given by the standard regression slope β_{21} of X_2 on X_1.

The derivation of estimates of p_{31} and p_{32} is only slightly complicated by the presence of two independent variables, X_1 and X_2, in the structural equation for X_3. Let us first multiply this structural equation, given by equation (3) above, through by X_1, obtaining

$$X_1X_3 = X_1(p_{31}X_1 + p_{32}X_2 + p_{3v}R_v)$$

(10)

$$= p_{31}X_1{}^2 + p_{32}X_1X_2 = p_{3v}X_1R_v.$$

If we now take the expectation of both sides of this equation, we have

$$E(X_1X_3) = E(p_{31}X_1{}^2 + p_{32}X_1X_2 + p_{3v}X_1R_v)$$

(11)

$$= p_{31}E(X_1{}^2) + p_{32}E(X_1X_2) + p_{3v}E(X_1R_v).$$

Since our variates are in standard form, $E(X_1X_3) = r_{13}$, $E(X_1{}^2) = 1$, and $E(X_1X_2) = r_{12}$. And since we have assumed, in equation (4) above, that R_v is uncorrelated with X_1, we may delete $p_{3v}E(X_1R_v)$ as having a vanishing value. Hence, (11) simplifies to an equation,

(12) $r_{13} = p_{31} + p_{32}r_{12},$

giving a relation between the parameters p_{31} and p_{32} in terms of two observed correlations, r_{12} and r_{13}. The two unknown parameters cannot be estimated from this one equation alone. But we may also multiply the structural equation for X_3 through by the second of its independent variables, X_2, obtaining

(13) $X_2X_3 = p_{31}X_1X_2 + p_{32}X_2{}^2 + p_{3v}X_2R_v.$

By taking the expectation of each side of this equation, we obtain

(14) $E(X_2X_3) = p_{31}E(X_1X_2) + p_{32}E(X_2^2) + p_{3v}E(X_2R_v)$.

By availing ourselves once again of the properties of variates in standard form and the restrictions on the error term, we may simplify equation (14) to a form,

(15) $r_{23} = p_{31}r_{12} + p_{32}$,

which also gives a relation between the parameters p_{31} and p_{32} in terms of two observed correlations. Having obtained two equations, (12) and (15), in these two unknowns, we may now solve for each parameter,[5] obtaining the following estimates:

(16) $p_{31} = \dfrac{r_{13} - r_{12}r_{23}}{1 - r_{12}^2}$

(17) $p_{32} = \dfrac{r_{23} - r_{12}r_{13}}{1 - r_{12}^2}$

These expressions are identical to the formulas for the standard partial regression coefficients $\beta_{31.2}$ and $\beta_{32.1}$.

We have, finally, to estimate the parameters of the structural equation for our third endogenous variate, X_4, as given by equation (5) above. Multiplying this equation through by X_2, taking expectations, and interpreting the resulting terms as we did above, we obtain the equation

(18) $r_{24} = p_{42} + p_{43}r_{23}$.

Similarly, by multiplying the structural equation for X_4 through by X_3, taking expectations, and interpreting the resulting terms, we obtain the equation

(19) $r_{34} = p_{42}r_{23} + p_{43}$.

Therefore, we again have two equations which may be solved for their two unknowns, giving these estimates:

(20) $p_{42} = \dfrac{r_{24} - r_{23}r_{34}}{1 - r_{23}^2} = \beta_{42 \cdot 3}$

(21) $p_{43} = \dfrac{r_{34} - r_{23}r_{24}}{1 - r_{23}^2} = \beta_{43 \cdot 2}$

[5] Provided the equations are linearly independent. The pattern of observed correlations might be such that the two equations in fact give only a single relation between the two unknown parameters, making it impossible to solve for their values without additional information. For this reason a formal statement of the conditions under which a model is identifiable would include the requirement that the matrix of coefficients of the estimating equations (correlation coefficients here) have a nonvanishing determinant of a given rank.

These are not the only estimation equations we might write for p_{42} and p_{43}, however. We noted above that the restrictions placed on the residual term, R_w, imply that this term is uncorrelated with X_1 as well as with X_2 and X_3. This has the interesting consequence that if we now multiply the structural equation for X_4 through by X_1, take expectations, and interpret the resulting terms, we obtain yet a third equation

$$(22) \qquad r_{14} = p_{42}r_{12} + p_{43}r_{13}$$

giving a relation between the parameters p_{42} and p_{43} in terms of certain of the observed correlations. Since only two equations are required to estimate these two unknowns, we have an embarrassment of riches. It is by no means mathematically necessary that the three pairs of equations we might choose from among the three equations (18), (19), and (22) will give consistent estimates of the unknown parameters. Their consistency is an open empirical question. Indeed, the answer to this question supplies a partial check on the validity of certain of our assumptions, particularly the independence of the disturbance terms and the absence of a term for X_1 from the structural equation for X_4. The Simon-Blalock technique "tests" the adequacy of a causal model by exploiting just this sort of overdetermination in the system of estimating equations.

An equivalent means of making this test is to rewrite the structural equation for X_4 so that it includes a term for X_1:

$$(23) \qquad X_4 = p_{41}X_1 + p_{42}X_2 + p_{43}X_3 + p_{4w}R_w.$$

With such a term added, the parameters of the structural equation for X_4 are now exactly determined: by multiplying equation (23) through successively by X_1, X_2, and X_3, taking expectations, and interpreting the resulting terms, we obtain three equations giving a relation among the three unknown parameters, p_{41}, p_{42}, and p_{43}, in terms of observed correlations. The test of our assumption that a term for X_1 can be deleted from this equation without loss of information lies of course in the value obtained for p_{41}. A negligible value of p_{41} would be consistent with our assumption that no arrow links X_1 with X_4 directly; a nonvanishing value would cause us to look again at the assumptions of our model. In the case of my illustrative example, p_{41} did not in fact exceed $+0.01$.[6]

---

[6] A vanishing estimate of this parameter would not of course validate all assumptions of the model. It would in particular give no information about the correctness of the direction in which several of the arrows are drawn, a point stressed by Wright which any working investigator would do well to keep in

How may values be given the coefficients we have associated with the residual factors R_u, R_v, and R_w? A simple extension of our method will yield these as well. Let us see how we might estimate p_{4w}, the coefficient representing influences on the Member's behavior which arise outside the model. We proceed by multiplying the structural equation for X_4 through by the only two factors appearing there which have not already been used for this purpose, R_w and X_4 itself. When we multiply through by R_w and take expectations, we obtain the equation

$$(24) \quad E(X_4R_w) = p_{42}E(X_2R_w) + p_{43}E(X_3R_w) + p_{4w}E(R_w{}^2).$$

The restrictions on R_w allow us to say that the first two terms on the right side of equation (24) will vanish. Since X_4 and (by assumption) R_w are scored in standard form, $E(X_4R_w) = r_{4w}$ and $E(R_w{}^2) = 1$. Hence, equation (24) simplifies to

$$(25) \qquad\qquad r_{4w} = p_{4w}.$$

This relation is not of direct aid in evaluating p_{4w} since R_w is unmeasured and r_{4w} unobserved. But if we multiply the structural equation for X_4 through by X_4 itself and take expectations, we obtain a further relation between r_{4w} and p_{4w} in terms of quantities which we can either observe or estimate: [7]

$$(26) \quad E(X_4{}^2) = p_{42}E(X_2X_4) + p_{43}E(X_3X_4) + p_{4w}E(X_4R_w)$$

$$(27) \qquad\qquad 1 = p_{42}r_{24} + p_{43}r_{34} + p_{4w}r_{4w}$$

If we substitute p_{4w} for r_{4w} in equation (27), as equation (25) says we may, and rearrange terms, we obtain:

$$(28) \qquad\qquad p_{4w}{}^2 = 1 - p_{42}r_{24} - p_{43}r_{34}$$

$$(29) \qquad\qquad p_{4w} = \sqrt{1 - p_{42}r_{24} - p_{43}r_{34}}.$$

A comparison of the estimated parameters for a given structural equation may be of high substantive interest. In this illustrative case

---

mind. For a discussion of this point, see Hugh Donald Forbes and Edward R Tufte, "A Note of Caution in Causal Modeling," *American Political Science Review,* LXII (December, 1968), 1258–64.

[7] This is of course a well-known relation in regression theory. Indeed, the coefficient of multiple determination of X_4 by X_2 and X_3 would be defined as $R_{4.32}^2 = 1 - p_{4w}r_{4w} = p_{42}r_{24} + p_{43}r_{34} = \beta_{42.3}r_{24} + \beta_{43.2}r_{34}$. It follows from this that $\sqrt{1 - R_{4.32}^2}$ provides an estimate of p_{4w} which is more convenient than that given by equation (29) below if the multiple correlation coefficient or its square has already been calculated.

the estimated values of the parameters of the equation for X_4 were
as follows:

(30) $p_{42} = +0.61$
(31) $p_{4w} = +0.51$
(32) $p_{43} = +0.33.$

These values imply that the Congressman's perception of his constituency's views was foremost among the immediate influences on
his behavior in this policy area. The manifold influences on his behavior arising outside the model were next in importance, with the
Congressman's own inclinations coming a rather poor third.

No one familiar with the interest shown by students of American
politics in the forces acting on the legislator could miss the relevance
of these findings to a standard problem of political analysis. Yet these
estimates cannot answer the question from which this study began.
The Congressman could vote in complete accord with his perception
of the constituency and yet further the constituency's influence not
at all if his perception of its views were wholly unreliable. Likewise,
he could give only moderate weight to his own beliefs and yet partially express the constituency's will if his own and the constituency's
views were wholly the same. To probe these indirect influences we
must do more than resolve the Congressman's behavior into a set of
immediate forces. We must combine the elementary path coefficients
of our model to estimate the importance of compound pathways of
influence.

The Analysis Of Compound Paths

In helping to solve a problem of this kind path analysis plays the
opposite of its classical role in genetic studies. A simple physical
analogy may clarify this difference. Let us think of our four-variable
model as describing a system of interlocking waterways along which
we have stationed observers to report on the level of the water at
four points, corresponding to $X_1, \ldots, X_4$. Water flows in a known
direction between each pair of points, the flow being regulated by a
gate between. The settings of the gates play the role of the elementary
path coefficients or parameters of the structural equations.

In the original, "direct" use of path analysis the investigator knew
the settings of the gates and deduced from these the relationships
that would be observed between the water levels at various points of
the system. In the familiar example of studies of inbreeding, the ge-
neticist knows the settings of the gates from Mendelian theory and
deduces the correlation of genetic characteristics that will be observed

between siblings after inbreeding has continued a given number of generations.

In the "inverse" use of path analysis the settings of the gates are unknown. The investigator begins instead with the correlations observed within the system and deduces what the settings of the gates must be in order to yield his observed data. This was the situation of the investigators in my illustrative case. We knew the intercorrelations of the observations at $X_1, \ldots, X_4$ and were willing to make certain assumptions about the direction of flow between points. From these we had to deduce the flows over the three distinct courses which link X_1 with X_4.

It seems intuitively clear that the amount of the flow over the whole of such a course must bear a multiplicative relationship to the amount of the flow past the individual gates along the way. No water will cover the whole of a particular course if any one of its gates is fully shut. And the flow over the whole of a course will be at a maximum when the flow past each of its gates is at a maximum. This intuition can be given mathematical foundation by putting in reduced form the structural equation for the variate which lies at the end of the course. Whenever a variate that is endogenous to a recursive system is partially determined by variates which are themselves endogenous, it is possible to put the structural equation for the variate which is "later" in the system in reduced form by substituting for the endogenous variates which are "earlier."

The application of this procedure to our illustrative case is completely straightforward. The structural equation for X_4 included two earlier endogenous variates, X_2 and X_3. Let us first of all use the relation given by the structural equation for X_3 (equation 3 above) to substitute for X_3 in the equation for X_4:

$$
\begin{aligned}
X_4 &= p_{42}X_2 + p_{43}(p_{31}X_1 + p_{32}X_2 + p_{3v}R_v) + p_{4w}R_w \\
(33) \quad &= p_{42}X_2 + p_{43}p_{31}X_1 + p_{43}p_{32}X_2 + p_{43}p_{3v}R_v + p_{4w}R_w \\
&= p_{43}p_{31}X_1 + (p_{42} + p_{43}p_{32})X_2 + p_{43}p_{3v}R_v + p_{4w}R_w.
\end{aligned}
$$

In this partially reduced form the equation for X_4 still includes an endogenous variate, X_2, which is later in the system than X_1. Let us therefore use the relation given by the structural equation for X_2 (equation 1 above) to reduce equation (33) still further:

$$
\begin{aligned}
X_4 &= p_{43}p_{31}X_1 + (p_{42} + p_{43}p_{32})(p_{21}X_1 + p_{2u}R_u) \\
&\quad + p_{43}p_{3v}R_v + p_{4w}R_w \\
&= p_{43}p_{31}X_1 + p_{42}p_{21}X_1 + p_{43}p_{32}p_{21}X_1 \\
(34) \quad &\quad + (p_{42}p_{2u} + p_{43}p_{32}p_{2u})R_u + p_{43}p_{3v}R_v + p_{4w}R_w \\
&= (p_{42}p_{21} + p_{43}p_{31} + p_{43}p_{32}p_{21})X_1 \\
&\quad + (p_{42}p_{2u} + p_{43}p_{32}p_{2u})R_u + p_{43}p_{3v}R_v + p_{4w}R_w.
\end{aligned}
$$

Equation (34) shows that X_4 can be written as a linear combination in which X_1 enters three times, each time with a weight equal to the product of the elementary path coefficients associated with one of the possible traverses between X_1 and X_4. This equation also shows that the remaining portion of X_4 is a linear combination of the residual influences R_u, R_v, and R_w. Since these residual terms are assumed to be independent of X_1, they will not contribute to the correlation of X_1 with X_4. Indeed, we may make explicit what equation (34) and the restrictions on residuals imply about the manner in which the correlation of X_1 with X_4 is built up if we multiply this equation through by X_1

$$(35) \quad \begin{aligned} X_1 X_4 = {}& (p_{42}p_{21} + p_{43}p_{31} + p_{43}p_{32}p_{21})X_1{}^2 \\ &+ (p_{42}p_{2u} + p_{43}p_{32}p_{2u})X_1 R_u + p_{43}p_{3v}X_1 R_v + p_{4w}X_1 R_w, \end{aligned}$$

take expectations

$$(36) \quad \begin{aligned} E(X_1 X_4) = {}& (p_{42}p_{21} + p_{43}p_{31} + p_{43}p_{32}p_{21})E(X_1{}^2) \\ &+ (p_{42}p_{2u} + p_{43}p_{32}p_{2u})E(X_1 R_u) + p_{43}p_{3v}E(X_1 R_v) + p_{4w}E(X_1 R_w), \end{aligned}$$

and interpret the left-hand side of this equation as the correlation we wish to partition:

$$(37) \quad r_{14} = p_{42}p_{21} + p_{43}p_{31} + p_{43}p_{32}p_{21}.$$

Thus, the correlation between the constituency's opinion and the Member's behavior may be written as the sum of three terms which exactly correspond to the three alternative pathways of influence originally posited. Each term is the product of the elementary path coefficients associated with the individual steps in its respective pathway.

In this illustrative case the values estimated for these compound paths were as follows:

$$p_{42}p_{21} = +0.45$$
$$p_{43}p_{31} = +0.02$$
$$p_{43}p_{32}p_{21} = +0.15$$

Under the assumptions of our model, the correlation of constituency opinion with legislative voting on civil rights is mainly the result of the Member's acting in accord with his correct perception of the constituency's views. By contrast, no more than a small contribution is made either by the Member's acting in accord with private inclinations that agree with the constituency's views or by the Member's obeying inclinations that have been adjusted to his correct perception of his constituency's views.

Wright's inventiveness lay partly in seeing how an expression such as equation (37) could be written by inspection of the appropriate arrow diagram. His algorithm allows the investigator to represent any correlation of two variates in a recursive system as the sum of the product associated with each of the admissible traverses between the variates.[8] But the investigator may reach a surer understanding of the basis of these expressions by deriving them from the structural equations of his system. In some cases this may save him from error in discerning the compound paths linking two variates in an intricate system.

The derivation of compound paths I have illustrated here may readily be generalized to all recursive systems in which we may wish to analyze the paths linking a variate that is "earlier" to one that is "later" in the order of variates. It is useful to distinguish here between two different cases. The first is that in which the correlation of two variates is wholly the result of the influence, direct or indirect, of the earlier variate on the later. This is illustrated by the example I have examined in detail, since the correlation of X_1 with X_4 is built up entirely of the indirect effects of one on the other. In any case of this sort successive substitution will reduce the structural equation of the later variate to a form which exhibits this influence explicitly. If the variates are in standard form we may then multiply this reduced equation through by the earlier variate and display the elementary and compound paths of which the correlation of the two variates is built up.[9]

The second case is that in which the correlation of the earlier variate with the later is only partly the result of the influence of the first on the second and is partly the result of the common influence on both of still earlier variates of the system. In any case of this sort we may still reduce the structural equation for the later variate until the indirect influence of the earlier variate is explicitly exhibited

[8] An admissible traverse is a sequence of single-headed arrows (elementary paths) and double-headed arrows (unanalyzed correlations) connecting the variates which satisfies the following conditions: (1) the traverse must start forward only once: if it moves backward from one variate and then forward toward the other, it must not change direction again; if it starts forward from one variate it must not change direction at all; (2) it must pass through any given variate of the system only once; and (3) it must include no more than one unanalyzed correlation (double-headed arrow).

[9] Provided of course that we are willing to assume that the disturbances associated with the later variate and with all intervening variates are uncorrelated with the earlier variate.

and then multiply through by the earlier variate to display the elementary and compound paths of which the correlation of the two variates is partially built up. But since the correlation is in this case formed of more than these paths, we would have one or more additional terms which express the presence of common influences on both the earlier and later variates. If we were, for example, to augment our illustrative model by including a variate X_0 which partially determines both X_1 and X_4 directly (but does not directly determine X_2 or X_3) equation (37) would then include an additional term expressing this common influence on both variates.[10]

There is of course a third possible case, that in which the correlation of two variates within a recursive system is entirely the result of common influences on both and not at all of the influence of one on the other. In this case neither variate occurs "earlier" in the order of variates. Many of Wright's genetic applications were of this kind. For example, the correlation of genetic characteristics between siblings is entirely the result of their heritance from common forebears and not at all the result of the genetic influence of one sibling on the other. I shall not examine this case further, but the analysis of paths contributing to a given correlation would also proceed by operations on the structural equations of the variates involved.

The Relaxation of Assumptions

I have set out the logic and certain of the detailed calculations of the treatment of compound paths in terms of a simplified example. The example is faithful to many of the original applications in population genetics, where recursiveness is assured by the procreative relationship of generations and the independence of stochastic disturbances by physical randomizing processes. There is not space here for a full survey of the difficulties which confront the investigator when these simplifying assumptions must be relaxed, but it is appropriate to suggest some of the issues that would arise. I shall also say a word about the assumptions we have tacitly made as to errors of measurement.

One respect in which the structure of constituency influence may be nonrecursive has already been noted. The Member may allow his perception of the constituency's view to form his own outlook, given the

---

[10] In this case the reduced form of the structural equation for X_4 analogous to equation (34) above would include the added term $p_{40}X_0$ and the partition of r_{14} analogous to that given by equation (37) would include the added term $p_{40}r_{01}$. If we assume that the disturbance in X_1 is uncorrelated with X_0, this latter term would be equivalent to $p_{40}p_{01}$ and would represent the compound path $X_4 \leftarrow X_0 \rightarrow X_1$.

enormous potential sanctions which the constituency holds. But he may also allow his perception of the constituency's views to be formed by his own views. Influence might therefore move in both directions between the two intervening terms, X_2 and X_3, and we might extend the structural equation for X_2 by including a term for X_3:

$$(38) \qquad X_2 = P_{21}X_1 + P_{23}X_3 + P_{2u}R_u$$

We may see the difficulties which this puts in the way of the analysis if we reconsider the means by which we estimated the parameters of the structural equation for X_3. If X_2 were to depend upon X_3 it would no longer be possible to assume that the residual influences on X_3 represented by R_v are uncorrelated with X_2, since these disturbances would now be among the influences on X_2. Hence, if we were to follow the procedure for estimating the parameters of the structural equation for X_3 outlined above, the term $p_{3v}E(X_2R_v)$ could not be deleted from equation (14), and equation (15) would be left with a nuisance term, $p_{3v}r_{2v}$, on the right-hand side.

The method of instrumental variables provides a way around these difficulties if we can find additional variables which are causally prior to the reciprocally-linked variables but which do not influence both these variables directly. Such prior "instruments" allow us to multiply the structural equations only by variables which are uncorrelated with their disturbance terms. Let us see how we would proceed in our illustrative case.

If we introduced a prior variable, X_0, which affected X_2 but neither (directly) affected nor is affected by X_3, our diagram of constituency influence would include an arrow from X_0 to X_2 (though none from X_0 to X_3), as well as the arrows in each direction between X_2 and X_3 which have introduced an element of nonrecursiveness into the model:

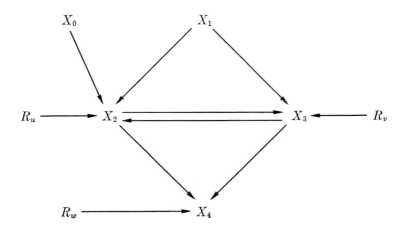

To estimate the parameters of the structural equation for X_3 we would now be able to multiply through by X_0 (as well as by X_1 as before) and take expectations. This would yield the added equation

$$(39) \qquad\qquad r_{03} = p_{31}r_{01} + p_{32}r_{02}$$

giving a relation between p_{31} and p_{32} in terms of certain observed correlations. Equation (39) with equation (12) would allow us to solve for the two unknown parameters. The success of this procedure rests on the fact that X_0, unlike X_2, does not depend on X_3; hence, the restriction $E(X_0R_v) = 0$ is not patently false. It also rests on the absence of a direct influence of X_0 on X_3; were we to posit such an influence, equation (39) would include a third unknown parameter, p_{30}, and we would be left with three unknowns to be estimated from only two equations. In like fashion, the estimation of the parameters of the new structural equation for X_2, equation (38) above, would depend on our being able to find an instrumental variable causally prior to X_2 and X_3 but without direct influence on X_2.

The formal neatness of such a solution should not mask the practical difficulties in finding instrumental variables which satisfy these conditions. It will often be particularly difficult to enforce the requirement that prior variables influence one but not both of the variates that are reciprocally linked. These difficulties were painfully real in the life history of the study which serves as my main example. The investigator who foresees nonrecursive elements in his system would do well to include in his research observations on several factors which are candidates for the role of instrumental variable. Indeed, research design, including the use of explicitly longitudinal designs where influence involves time, offers the best hope of solving the analytical problems posed by reciprocal causation and feedback loops. Elegant reanalysis is a poor remedy for opportunities missed at the stage of design.

In a nonrecursive system the correlation of two variates will not in general decompose into a sum of products of elementary path coefficients corresponding to the possible traverses between the variates. Hence, the compound path coefficients will not in general be products of elementary path coefficients. But we may derive valid equations partitioning the correlations of a nonrecursive system by reducing the structural equations and taking expectations in a way that is quite analogous to the operations I have set out above. Such an analysis can be equally revealing of the importance of various indirect causal linkages.[11]

[11] Interesting discussions of path analysis of nonrecursive systems appear in Malcolm E. Turner and Charles D. Stevens, "The Regression Analysis of Causal

The principal difficulty in the way of the path analysis of social and political structures may, however, be the frailty of the measurements that are typically available to the investigator. The most elementary consideration shows how easily random and nonrandom errors can distort estimates of the parameters of a structural model.[12] Indeed, these effects are serious enough to raise doubts about many of the tests of structural models which have utilized data of uncertain validity and reliability.

Certainly we have sensed the effect of measurement error in various of the results of the analysis which has served as my main example. In view of the probable error in measuring the Member's attitude and his perception of the constituency's attitude, we have looked upon a detailed quantity such as the vanishing estimate of p_{41} I have quoted above as being partly accidental, and this belief was strengthened by extending the analysis to two Congresses. Rather than place too fine an interpretation on individual estimates, we have tended to rest our conclusions on the broad contrasts to be seen in the estimates of compound paths obtained in the three issue domains included within this research. We discuss elsewhere our reasons for supposing that this increases the robustness of the findings against the distorting effects of errors of measurement.[13]

The problem posed by such errors must also be solved by elaborations of research design. In some types of research the investigator must of course work with the measures available to him. But in

---

Paths," *Biometrics,* XV (June, 1959), 236–58, and Sewall Wright, "The Treatment of Reciprocal Interaction, with or without Lag, in Path Analysis," *Biometrics,* XVI (September, 1960), 423–45. A vast econometrics literature deals with estimation in nonrecursive systems. An excellent recent survey of these problems is given by Franklin M. Fisher, "Dynamic Structure and Estimation in Economy-wide Econometric Models," ch. 15 in James S. Dusenberry *et al.* (eds.), *The Brookings Quarterly Econometric Model of the United States* (Chicago, Ill.: Rand McNally, 1965), pp. 589–635.

[12] Hubert Blalock has written an excellent series of papers on measurement error in causal inference. See in particular, "Making Causal Inferences for Unmeasured Variables from Correlations among Indicators," *American Journal of Sociology,* LXIX (July, 1963), 53–62, "Some Implications of Random Measurement Error for Causal Inferences," *American Journal of Sociology,* LXXI (July, 1965), 37–47, "Multiple Indicators and the Causal Approach to Measurement Error," *American Journal of Sociology,* LXXV (September, 1969), 264–72, and an unpublished paper with Caryll S. Wells and Lewis S. Carter, "The Statistical Estimation of Random Measurement Error." See also Paul M. Siegel and Robert W. Hodge, "A Causal Approach to the Study of Measurement Error," in Hubert M. Blalock and Ann B. Blalock (eds.), *Methodology in Social Research* (New York: McGraw-Hill, 1969), 28–59, and Herbert L. Costner, "Theory, Deduction, and Rules of Correspondence," *American Journal of Sociology,* LXXV (September, 1969), 245–63.

[13] Miller and Stokes, *The Structure of Representation.*

others he has considerable latitude in designing his measures. This is specifically true of those who practice the survey arts. We may expect a growing realization of the effects of uncertain measurements to inspire a more systematic study of error.

One consequence of this will be the development of measures which are freer of error. But it is unlikely that salvation will lie in this direction alone. An equally important consequence is likely to be that investigators will measure their error well enough to include its effects explicitly in more complex but more realistic structural models. In this sense the frailties of empirical measures make the need for simultaneous equation methods greater rather than less. If we are to overcome a principal obstacle to these methods giving worthwhile results across a broad range of studies, we shall need to combine better research design with the estimation of structural models which are increasingly complex.